BOOK
CASES

14 DIY DESIGNER PROJECTS

BOOK
CASES

FROM
SALVAGE
TO
STORAGE

AURÉLIE DROUET

Photography JÉRÔME BLIN

SCRIPTUM
EDITIONS

CONTENTS

DESIGNS

DESIGNER PROFILES

181 APPENDICES

INSPIRATIONS

INTRODUCTION

'When I think of all the books I haven't read yet, I know with certainty that I am a happy man.'
Jules Renard

I love books. I love everything about them, from their covers to the grain of their paper. I love them for their sheer beauty as things, from musty leather-bound tomes to the latest paperbacks. I like to mark my place by turning down the corner of a page. I like to arrange books on shelves and heap them in piles. I like to leave bookmarks in them to mark long-forgotten places. I like to re-read them. I love bookshops. In short, I love books.

I also love their natural companion: the bookcase. Bookcases invite curious glances and closer inspection, both for what they contain and for what they are. As reflections of their owners' tastes, they are highly personal. From meticulously organized displays to shelves groaning under the weight of random volumes, from the classic and formal to the decorative and eclectic, every bookcase is unique.

Bookcases are major players in any room. With their lines and dimensions, they structure the volume and influence our perception of the space. The choice of a bookcase requires some reflection. Flat-pack or bespoke? Imposing or discreet? Wood or metal? While some factors are non-negotiable, such as the height and depth of the shelves, others offer free rein for the imagination. Materials, shapes and colours can all be as quirky and creative as you care to make them.

This book is filled with ideas for displaying and organizing your books, from designer creations to architectural visions. All of them are simple enough to make at home, using methods of construction and assembly that have been carefully devised to be as accessible as possible. Whether stretched the length of a wall or tucked under the stairs, standing on the floor or hung on the wall, static or movable, these varied designs show that bookcases can be created in all shapes and sizes, for the pleasure and convenience of book-lovers of every persuasion.

TIPS AND POINTERS

To build the designs

For each design you will find a list of the tools and materials required to make it. As the basic toolkit is not repeated each time, here is a list of the tools that you will need to keep to hand: :

- tape measure
- good quality carpenter's pencil
- metal rule and set square
- gloves, safety goggles and mask
- flat and Phillips screwdrivers
- hammers (various sizes),
- pliers (various)
- paintbrushes and rollers (various types and sizes)

Measurements for nails, screws and nuts are for guidance only, to be adapted according to the thickness of the boards and the material of the wall (wood, stone, plasterboard etc.)

To create your own designs

All the designs suggested here are basic models from which you can improvise your own designs.

Be imaginative!

Readers are invited to send photographs of their own designs inspired by this book to the author at: aureliedrouet@free.fr

A GLOSSARY OF THINGS BOOKISH ...

Some key terms from the world of books explained:

AI Abbreviation for Advance Information (Sheet), a document produced by publishers for new titles.

ANTHOLOGY A collection of writings from a variety of authors/sources.

ART/COFFEE TABLE BOOK High quality illustrated books.

BOOKBINDING The process of binding a book, which may include folding and sewing the pages and attaching the cover. Modern books may have either a hardback or a paperback binding

BOOK DESIGNER Person who designs the appearance of a book according to the publisher's specifications.

BERNE CONVENTIONS An international agreement made in 1886 for the respect of copyright between participating nations.

BLAD A term used to describe a form of advance sales material consisting of a selection of pages of text and illustrations wrapped inside a proof of the book jacket.

BLEED A term used for an illustration or image which extends beyond the trimmed page.

BLOCKING/CASE STAMPING The use of metallic foils on the spine of a hardback book.

BLURB The brief description of a book which appears on the back or front flap of a book.

BOOK BLOCK The sewn or perfect bound pages of a hardback book before they are cased in.

BULK The thickness of a book.

CASED/HARDBACK Derived from the case into which the book block is inserted (cased in) when bound.

COMMISSIONING EDITOR A person employed in a publishing house to seek out authors to write particular books for publication.

COPY EDITOR The person employed in a publishing house who works on the detail of a book, ensuring accuracy and completeness and preparing it for typesetting.

CROWN OCTAVO Book format, trimmed page size 189 x 123 mm sewn (120 mm unsewn).

CROWN QUARTO Book format, trimmed page size 246 x 189 mm, frequently an economical choice for illustrated books.

DEMY OCTAVO Book format, trimmed page size 216 x 138 mm sewn (135 mm unsewn).

DUES Orders taken before a title is published, or while it is for any reason unavailable, which are fulfilled when stock is available. Called 'back orders' in the US.

ENDPAPERS The pages of heavy cartridge paper at the front and back of a hardback book. Often coloured, or patterned.

FIRST EDITION First printing of a book.

FOLIO The page number which is printed at the top or bottom of each page.

FORE-EDGE The right-hand edge of a book when opened, opposite the spine.

FRONTISPIECE An illustration inserted to face the title-page.

HALF-TITLE The first page of a book, on which the title is displayed.

HEADBAND A decorative strip of coloured material glued to the top of the spine of the book block of a hardback. Usually used in conjunction with a tailband.

IMPOSITION The positioning of pages on a sheet, or reel of paper, which when printed and folded into sections produce the correct sequence of pages.

IMPRINT The name of the publisher under which a title is issued. Large publishing houses may have more than one imprint.

JACKET Removable cover designed to protect a hardback or paperback binding.

LAYOUT Page by page design of a book, usually done on a computer.

LICENCE A subsidiary right usually granted for a fixed term or for a particular usage by the holder of the head contract in a work.

LITERARY AGENT A person or company looking after the interests of author clients and managing the exploitation of rights in an author's work.

MARKETING The department in a publishing house with responsibility for promoting published titles .

MONOCHROME Printing in one colour, usually black.

NET BOOK AGREEMENT The agreement whereby publishers in the UK were able to dictate the minimum retail price; abandoned in the UK 1995, but still exists in some countries.

OP Universal abbreviation for Out of Print.

OZALIDS/BLUES A form of proof used to check the position of text and illustrations as a final stage of approval before printing.

PACKAGER A company which creates and originates, sometimes manufactures, books for publishers.

PAGE PROOF A low-quality print out of the pages in a book, often used not only to check accuracy of typesetting but also as an advance promotional tool.

PAPER ENGINEERING The devising of the mechanics of novelty books and pop-up books.

PERFECT BOUND Adhesive binding in which the individual pages of a book are glued together as opposed to section sewn.

PICTURE RESEARCH The process of finding suitable illustrations to the text of a book.

POINT SIZE A measurement for type.

PREFACE OR FOREWORD Introductory address to the reader, sometimes written by someone other than the author.

PRELIMS Abbreviation for the preliminary pages of a book before the start of the main text.

PRINT RUN The number of copies printed in a single printing.

PROCESS COLOURS The four colour colours used in printing to represent the full spectrum: cyan, yellow, magenta and black.

PRODUCTION The department within a publishing house responsible for print and paper buying and cost and quality control.

PROOFREADER A person who reads text proofs to ensure accuracy.

PUBLISHER Person or company whose principal activity is the production and marketing of books.

RECTO The right-hand page of an opening in a book.

REMAINDERS A publisher's overstock sold off cheaply.

REPRINT A second or subsequent printing of a title with minimal alteration to the text.

REPRO A common abbreviation for the reproduction of illustrations; a company carrying out such work is called a 'repro house'.

ROYAL OCTAVO Book format, 234 x 156 mm (153 mm unsewn), very common in all sectors of the market.

ROYALTY The payment made by publishers to authors, and others, on sales made; typically a percentage of the recommended retail price.

RUNNING HEAD The line which commonly appears at the top of each printed page, typically showing the book title on the left-hand side and chapter title on the right.

SALE OR RETURN The arrangement whereby books supplied by publishers to booksellers may be returned for credit if subsequently unsold.

SERIES A sequence of books sharing certain characteristics and published by the same publisher.

SIGNATURES Printers' term for sections of a book.

SLIPCASE A cardboard box open at one end into which a book (or two or three volumes) are inserted.

SPINE The part of a book that is visible when it is stored on a bookshelf.

TAILBANDS A decorative strip of coloured material glued to the bottom of the spine of the book block of a hardback. Always used in conjunction with a headband.

TITLE-PAGE The page, normally the second leaf in a book, which displays the title, author and publisher's name.

TYPEFACE/FONT The design/style of the individual characters making up the text of a book.

VERSO The reverse of a page in a book, thus the left-hand page of an opening.

WOODFREE Paper made from chemically treated woodpulp and used for good quality book production because of its colour fastness and durability.

1.

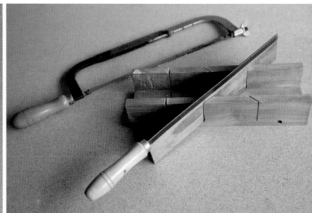

2.

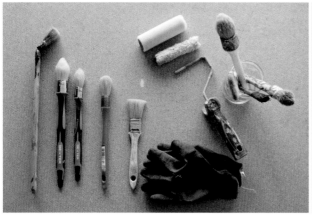

3.

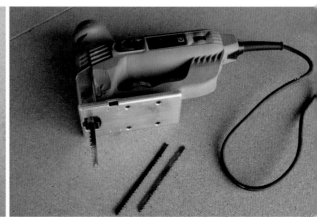

4.

5.

6.

TOOL GUIDE

Basic protective equipment (1)

The use of gloves, a mask (even for sanding) and sometimes safety glasses is seriously recommended. This basic equipment is indispensable for protecting the hands and face when using certain tools and handling chemical products. We also advise using products that respect the environment, and that will consequently also respect the user's health.

Mitre box (2)

U-shaped in section, with notches for making 45-degree and 90-degree cuts, the mitre box is an indispensable tool for carpentry. Although the tenon saw (hacksaw) is associated with this tool, a handsaw with a blade fine enough to fit in the notches can also be used. Position the piece of wood in the box and hold it firmly in place, then slide the saw blade into the notches to either side of it, according to the angle you want to achieve.

Paintbrushes and rollers (3)

Brushes are available in different sizes and materials for different uses. For fiddly jobs such as cutting in, we recommend using a sash brush, which is pointed.[see note about brushes above] Flat brushes are used for varnishing and lacquering. For varnishing or painting large flat surfaces, use a mini-roller. The end result you obtain will depend on your choice of paintbrush or roller, so don't hesitate to seek professional advice when buying.

Jigsaw (4)

To ensure that you get the best use out of your jigsaw, make sure you choose one that can cut different thicknesses of wood, and has variable speeds and an adjustable base plate (up to 45 degrees) for making cuts on sloping surfaces. Choose the right blade for the material you want to saw. Observe the necessary safety precautions, and the jigsaw will help you to work accurately and safely.

Eccentric sander (5)

The eccentric sander has a rotating circular sanding surface designed for both coarse and fine sanding for a perfect finish. Light and easy to handle, it can be used on all surfaces except corners. Wear a dust mask, gloves and safety glasses, and always sand along the grain. When a surface is properly sanded it should be smooth to the touch.

Detail sander (6)

The detail or corner sander is a vibrating sander that is ideal for finishing. The shape and small dimensions of its sanding surface make it highly practical for sanding small areas that are flat but 'distressed', and for reaching awkward spots, and it is both light and very easy to use.

I READ THEREFORE I AM

DESIGN

100% recycled! An unwanted ladder metamorphoses into a bookshelf. Rescued from a junkyard in its original state, it still bears the marks of its past.

All it needed was a good clean, to preserve its natural patina and authentic charm.

DESIGN:
DENIS GUITTON

I READ THEREFORE I AM

TOOLBOX	
Tools	**Materials**
• Soda crystals (washing soda) • Brush • Square • Handsaw • Medium-grit sandpaper • Screw gun • Spirit level • Paintbrushes	• Ladder (here *4.7m (15'5") long*) • 10 mounting brackets *90(5½") x 50(2") x 50mm(2")* • Single-thread multipurpose woodscrews • Screws and rawlplugs appropriate for your wall • Dark grey metal primer and top coat

Telling details: the ladder before and after cleaning (left), and the visible mounting brackets (right) which complement room's colour scheme.

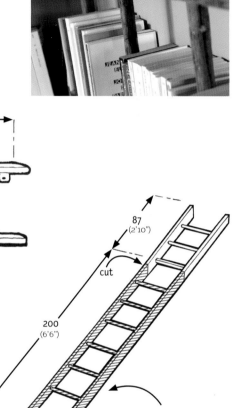

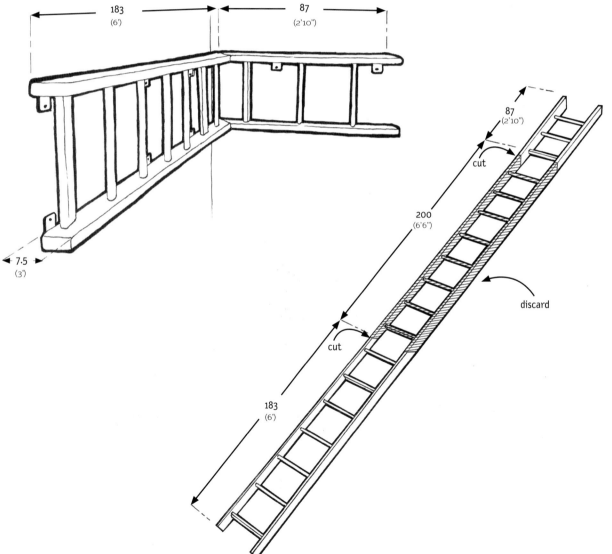

183
(6')

87
(2'10")

7.5
(3')

87
(2'10")

cut

200
(6'6")

discard

cut

183
(6')

All measurements are given in centimetres and inches (to nearest fraction).

Step-by-step-guide

1. Clean the ladder using a brush and soda crystals dissolved in hot water (50$_g$/.9^{oz} per litre/pint).

2. Working from one end of the ladder, measure and mark off the required length (here 185cm (6'1")) on the side rail, drawing a perpendicular pencil line.

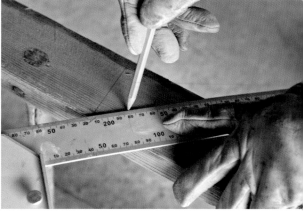

3. To cut the uprights at an angle, measure the width of the upright, then measure the same distance from the perpendicular line.

4. Draw in the diagonal between these two marks.

5. Use a handsaw to saw along the diagonal. Repeat this process starting from the other end of the ladder, so retaining both ends (see diagram).

6. Use sandpaper to smooth off the cut surfaces.

7. Position the two sections to make a corner, then drill pilot holes to prevent the wood from splitting.

8. Assemble the two sections using wood screws.

Step-by-step-guide

9. Paint the mounting brackets with metal paint.

10. Attach the brackets to the outside of the uprights (3 on the longer side, 2 on the shorter), so that they will sit underneath the finished bookshelves.

11. Attach 5 brackets to the inside of the uprights, facing the ones on the outside.

12. Touch over the screw heads with the metal paint.

13. Using a spirit level to check it is horizontal, fix the ends of the ladder using screws and rawlplugs suitable for your wall.

14. Once the ladder is straight, screw the rest of the brackets to the wall.

15. To ensure your books stay in place, take care over the gap you leave between the ladder and the wall. Measure the width of the books you want to accommodate in order to work out the position of the brackets.

Denis Guitton
Designer and innovator

Art lover, secondhand dealer, designer, handyman, inventor – Denis Guitton is a man of many talents, hard to pin down. With a grandfather who was a rag-and-bone man and an uncle who was an antique dealer, recycling is in his blood, and he started dealing in secondhand goods from an early age. Not content with merely buying and selling, however, he is also an innovator. It is not so much the objects themselves as their history that fascinates him. He combines his passion for anything old with design projects based on salvage and recycling, with a particular interest in wood – like a modern-day Geppetto.

How did you start designing bookcases?
For me, a bookcase is not so much a shrine as a gallery. At a single glance, books can tell you so much. I like ideas that are simple and unusual. A bookcase welcomes you into a room and gives you something to look it. The bookcase itself and the books that it holds are just as important as each other.

What has inspired you in your designs?
I love libraries, and especially the Biblioteca Laurenziana, the Medici library in Florence. As I buy and sell secondhand objects for a living, my designs are inspired by salvaged pieces. A dresser top, a ladder or some scaffolding might all be turned into bookcases. When you're salvaging and recycling you need to be able to look at things a different way, to have new ideas. There are no limits to the ideas our imagination can create, it's just up to us to work out how to put them into practice.

What are your tips for making a bookcase?
Avoid a linear approach, and give the books room to breathe. Make the shelves of different heights, display the books as though they were sculptures, include some of your favourite objects. The bookcase should be a 'living' thing, brought to life by books and objects.

Tell us some of your favourite books.
Two books have made a particular impression on me: *Fables*, by Loqman 'Le Sage' (Imprimerie de la République, year XI-1803), and *Les Racines du ciel*, by Romain Gary (Gallimard, English translation: *The Roots of Heaven* by Time, Inc in 1964).

Denis Guitton
Beaupuy - 85480 Fougeré, France
Tél. : +33 (0) 6 64 24 76 60 - guittondenis@yahoo.fr

I read therefore I am (p.16)

1, 2, 3 ...
MY FIRST BOOKCASE!

DESIGN

Reading doesn't have to be complicated: a love of books can start very early when you have your own bookcase. A little corner of your room where you can escape into the world of words.

This design makes it easy for children to put their books away. And having the front covers facing outwards makes it easy for them to choose the book they want to read.

Shush, they're reading ...

DESIGN:
FANNY MERCIER

1, 2, 3 ... MY FIRST BOOKCASE!

TOOLBOX

Tools

- Set square
- Straight edge
- Tape measure
- Masking tape
- Handsaw
- Screw gun
- Spirit level
- Paintbrushes

Materials

- 2 2.5m (8'2") timber battens, 28(2") x 28mm (2")
- 9 screws ø6 ($^{15}/_{64}$) x 70mm (2¾") + rawlplugs suitable for your wall
- 6 screw eyes ø4.5 (³/₁₆) x 35mm (1³/₈") + rawlplugs suitable for your wall
- 8m (26') ø4mm (⁵/₃₂) coloured nylon braided elastic cord
- Acrylic paint in the colour of your choice

 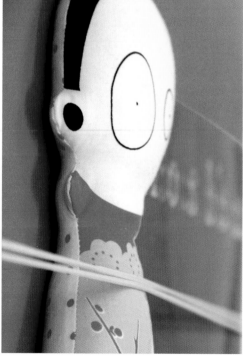

Telling details: Brightly coloured nylon cord and paint make
a cheerful colour scheme for a child's bedroom.

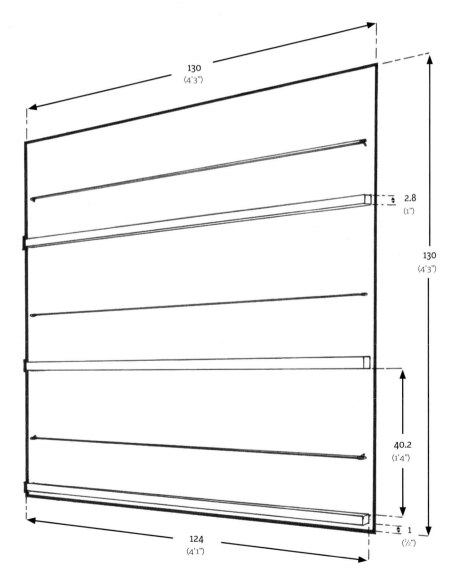

130
(4'3")

2.8
(1")

130
(4'3")

40.2
(1'4")

124
(4'1")

1
(½")

All measurements are given in centimetres and inches (to nearest fraction).

Step-by-step-guide

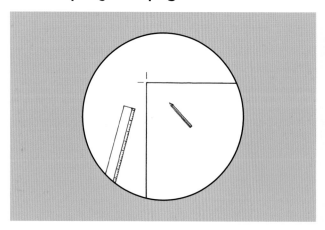

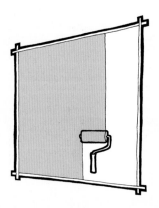

1. Using a straight edge and spirit level, mark out a 130 (4'3") x 130cm (4'3") square on the wall.

2. Stick masking tape around the edges of the square and paint inside it. As soon as you have finished, carefully remove the masking tape.

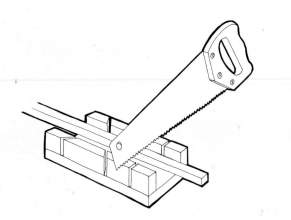

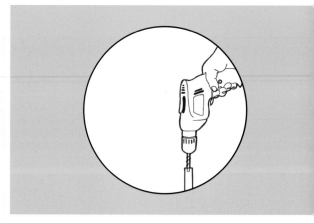

3. Saw the timber battens into 3 lengths of 124cm (4'1") and paint them.

4. Mark out the centre and ends of the battens, then drill pilot holes using a wood drill bit.

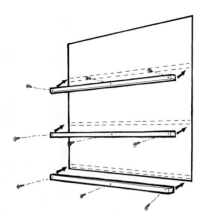

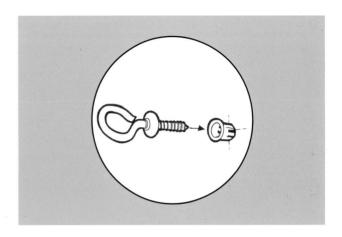

5. To mark out the positions of the screws, position each batten against the wall and pass the point of a pencil through the holes. Drill holes in the wall using a drill bit of the diameter indicated on the rawlplugs packet and insert the rawlplugs. Screw the battens to the wall. To finish off, touch over the screw heads with paint.

6. Screw in the eye screws and rawlplugs 15cm (6") above the battens.

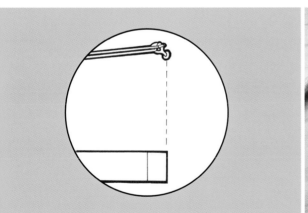

7. Cut the elastic cord in 3 and thread a double length between each pair of eye screws.

8. Red, yellow, blue, pink, white, mauve – braided elastic cord (available in haberdashery departments or on the internet) comes in a wide range of colours to complement your colour scheme.

MULTI-LAYERED READINGS

When architects Claire Escalon and Nicolas Lanno first saw this former printing works, built by Gustave Eiffel in the late nineteenth century, they were completely seduced by its 'open-plan layout, lofty ceilings and lightness'. It was love at first sight.

In their skilful use of the space, they have included dedicated spaces for books in every room.

DESIGN:
ATELIER PREMIER ÉTAGE

MULTI-LAYERED READINGS

'We haven't changed the configuration of the space. We've reorganized it by changing the way some of the walls look and adding numerous storage solutions, as these were completely lacking. We have masses of books, especially large illustrated editions. We didn't want an arrangement that would be too imposing or linear; instead we wanted to create lots of small spaces for reading. We used Batipin plywood sheets, a remarkable material that we like very much and that offers many advantages, both aesthetic and technical.'

CLOSE-UP ON MATERIALS

BATIPIN

Batipin is an environmentally friendly plywood made from maritime pine, with a pronounced grain that adds an extra dimension. This aesthetic quality, combined with its solidity and ease of use, makes it an ideal material for use in interior design. The thickness used here is 19mm (¾").

PLASTERBOARD

Consisting of an inner layer of gypsum sandwiched between lining paper of various weights and thicknesses, plasterboard is used for partitions and ceilings and to finish walls. The boards can be screwed to metal rails or a timber framework and the joins covered with tape and then plastered for a more aesthetic finish.

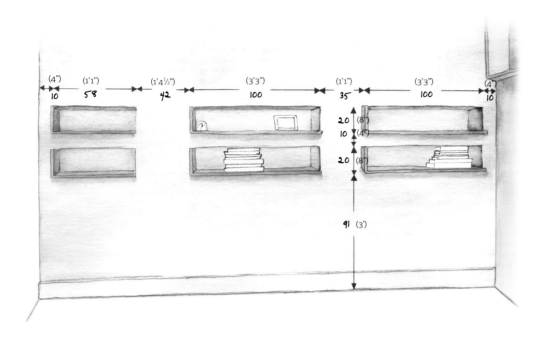

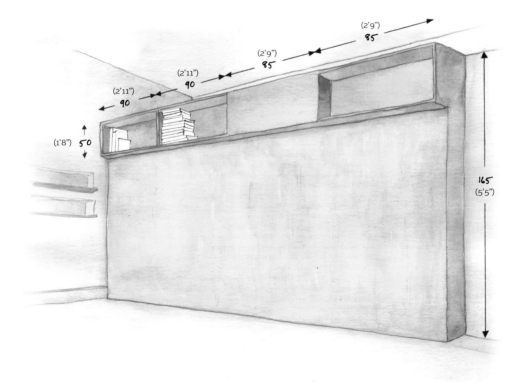

All measurements are given in centimetres and inches (to nearest fraction).

Construction

To maximize the available space, Claire and Nicolas opted for storage solutions that took up no floor space, creating plasterboard niches and a bookcase-wall in Batipin. These plywood sheets have a warm look and feel, while their grain adds visual interest to the room, 'like wallpaper'.

HORIZONTAL

The original wall between the sitting room and the bathroom has been replaced with a Batipin partition. Open at the top to reveal the ceiling, this has the visual effect of enlarging the space. The partition is topped off by a horizontal bookshelf, beneath which sits the sofa.

WALL NICHES

Claire and Nicolas have made use of the existing shallow niches in the sitting room to house coffee table books, using two sides of Batipin to make deeper spaces. The striations of the cut edges echo each other, emphasizing the perpendicular structural lines.

PAPERBACK CORNER

Making use of every nook and cranny, the architects created niches in the depth of the toilet wall. This can also be done in existing walls, but in this case locating the rails, cutting out and installing the plasterboard are all skilled jobs.

GLOBE READER

Imagine a set of bookcases with barely a vertical, horizontal or parallel line between them. Not just a book storage solution, *Globe Reader* is also a statement feature in its own right.

Arrange the separate elements however they best suit your space. Then fill the continents with books. Let your imagination take over. As Victor Hugo wrote: 'To read is to travel, to travel is to read.'

DESIGN:
JEAN-MARIE REYMOND

GLOBE READER

TOOLBOX

Tools

- Jigsaw
- Handsaw
- Rasp
- Screw gun
- Eccentric sander *(+ belt sander recommended)*
- Coarse, medium and fine-grit sandpaper
- Clamps
- Spatula
- Sash paintbrush
- Wide flat paintbrush

Materials

- 10 *2m(6' 6")* timber planks *18(¾") x 150mm(6")*
- Roll of tracing, or brown wrapping paper
- Single-thread multi-purpose wood screws
- Screws and rawlplugs appropriate for your wall
- 30 *3(1¼") x 3cm(1¼")* white epoxy L-brackets
- Wood glue
- Filler
- Paint in the colour of your choice
- Clear matt water-based varnish

Telling details: An adjustable design featuring separate
elements framed by broken lines, brought together to create a single image.

See the squared template on p.184

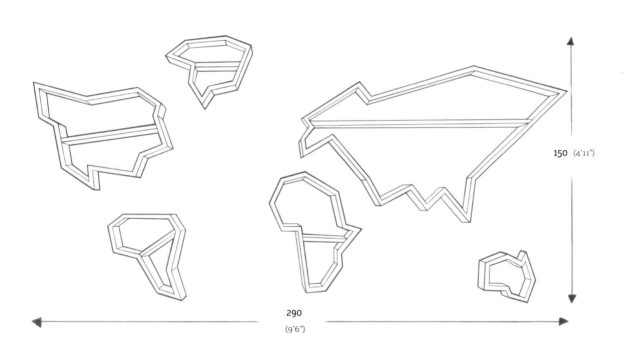

150 (4'11")

290
(9'6")

All measurements are given in centimetres and inches (to nearest fraction).

Step-by-step-guide

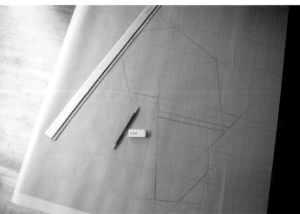

1. Sand the planks with an eccentric sander, starting with coarse-grit paper and finishing with medium-grit.
Tip: If you have a belt sander, use this in the first instance as the surface will be quite rough.

EXAMPLE : AFRICA

2. Mark out a large sheet of tracing paper in 10cm (4") squares, then draw the outline of the continent (here Africa) following the template on p. 184.
Tip: The shapes and sizes of the elements can be adapted to suit your space. Mark the paper in squares to the scale you want and draw in your own design.

3. Position a plank on the first section and mark the cuts on both sides. These will enable you to draw the angles of the cuts, which in this design vary in every case.

4. Mark the cutting line on both sides and across the thickness.

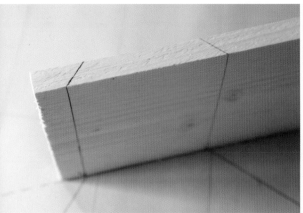

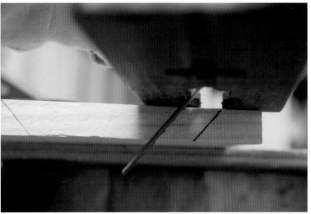

5. <u>NB</u>: As each section has two ends, the planks will also have two guide lines which may be different from each other.

6. Adjust the angle of the jigsaw blade to cut a chamfered edge.

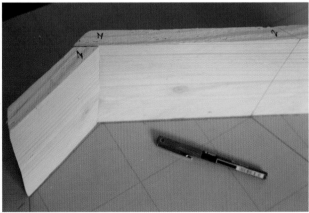

7. To finish off, sand the edges with coarse-grit sandpaper.

8. Reposition the first section on the template, then use the angle of the offcut from step 6 to make the second section. Mark the second guide line at the other end, then saw along it.

Step-by-step-guide

9. Glue the first two sections together and hold them in place with clamps.

10. Pre-drill pilot holes in both pieces of wood.

11. Screw the two pieces together.

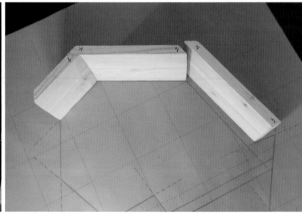

12. Using the template, repeat steps 3 to 11 to complete the outline and shelf

13. Saw or file off any excess or overhang at the joints.

14. Use filler to cover the screw heads. Use a spatula to fill the holes, then smooth off any surplus. When the filler is dry, sand it lightly with fine-grit sandpaper.

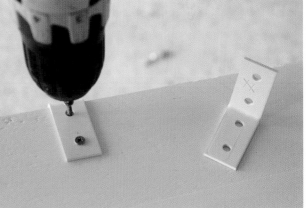

15. To paint the continents, use a flat brush for the flat surfaces and a sash brush for the internal angles and edges. To make the other continents, repeat steps 1 to 15.

16. To ensure each element can carry the weight of your books, screw several brackets to each continent outline and shelf. Fix these to the wall, using the appropriate screws and rawlplugs.

Treme-Treme
Triptyque/São Paulo-Paris

When the art and design connoisseur Houssein Jarouch commissioned Triptyque to design a 300-square-metre (3,300-sq-ft) apartment for him, the result was this remarkable space. The central striking feature is the curving 'Treme-Treme' bookcase, which wraps round the main living space and adds a vibrant sense of movement.

INSPIRED BY THE GRAPHIC OUTLINES OF SÃO PAULO'S CITY CENTRE TOWERS, THE LIBRARY IS A HOMAGE TO THE BRAŽILIAN MEGALOPOLIS.

MATERIAL: 9MM MDF, FINISHED WITH WHITE LACQUER.

Triptyque is a Franco-Brazilian architectural practice founded in 2000 by Grégory Bousquet, Carolina Bueno, Guillaume Sibaud and Olivier Raffaelli. With offices in São Paulo and Paris, it seeks solutions to the issues facing emerging towns and cities.

Triptyque
- 38, rue de Rochechouart
75009 Paris, France
Tel: 33 (0)1 75 43 42 16

- Al. Gabriel Monteiro da Silva,
484 - 01442-000 São Paulo, Brazil
Tel: + 55 11 30 81 35 65
www.triptyque.com

1. The central feature of the apartment, the library is a presence in every room.

2. A flat screen is discreetly integrated within the library's undulating contours.

SOMMAIRE SHELVES

DESIGN

Using threaded steel rods and natural pine,
Sommaire Shelves favours a minimalist approach.

Making use of the full height available, this unusual combination
of wood and steel offers a book storage solution that is both
simple to construct and easy to adapt.

DESIGN:
AURÉLIE DROUET

SOMMAIRE SHELVES

TOOLBOX	
<u>Tools</u>	<u>Materials</u>
■ Jigsaw ■ Hacksaw ■ Spanner ■ Drill with ø13mm(½) and ø15mm(37/64) wood bits ■ Eccentric drill ■ Detail sander ■ Clamps ■ Coarse and medium-grit sandpaper	■ 4 lengths rough-sawn pine 4.8m(15'9") x 2.7cm(1") x 30cm(1') ■ 24 1m(3'3") lengths of ø14mm(½") threaded steel rods ■ Packet of ø14mm(½") nuts and washers ■ 16 ø14mm(½") threaded joiners

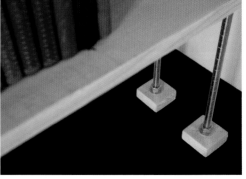

Telling details: natural wood and steel combine to make an
elegant design that is quick and easy to build.

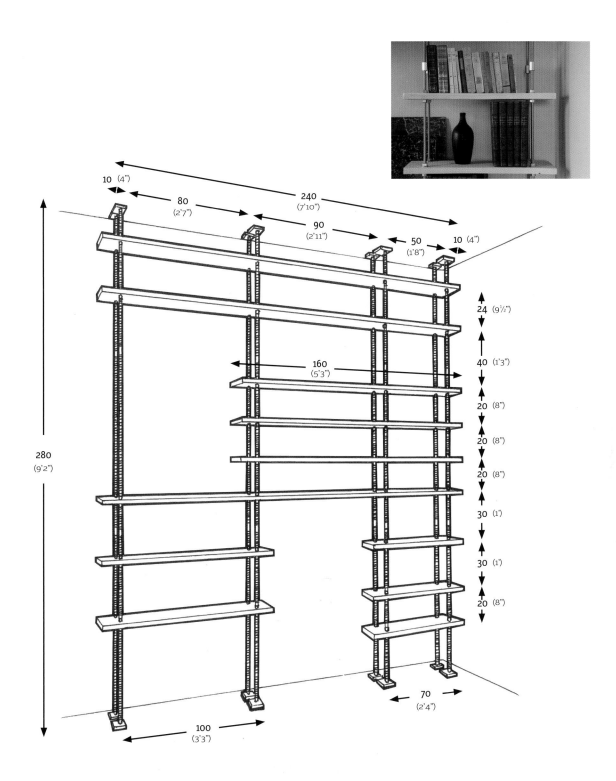

10 (4")

80
(2'7")

240
(7'10")

90
(2'11")

50
(1'8")

10 (4")

24 (9½")

40 (1'3")

160
(5'3")

20 (8")

20 (8")

20 (8")

280
(9'2")

30 (1')

30 (1')

20 (8")

70
(2'4")

100
(3'3")

All measurements are given in centimetres and inches (to nearest fraction).

Step-by-step-guide

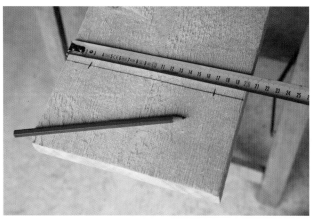

1. Mark out and saw the planks following the measurements given on the diagram. On one of the 2.4m (7'10") lengths, mark the positions of the threaded rods.

2. Drill the holes using a wood bit slightly wider in diameter than the steel rod, here 15mm ($^{37}/_{64}$). This plank will serve as the template for all the other holes.

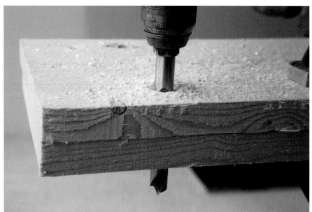

3. Position a second plank precisely under the drilled plank and clamp in place. Drill the holes. Repeat this process with all the other planks, being careful to position the steel rods according to the length of the plank.

4. Sand all the planks, starting with a coarse-grit sandpaper and finishing with a medium.

5. Use a detail sander to round off the edges.

6. Using an offcut, cut 16 blocks, 6.5 (2½") x 6.5cm (2½"), to attach to the ends of the steel rods.

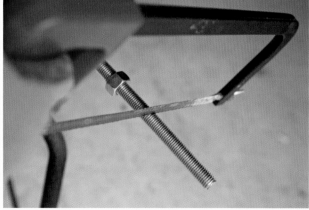

7. Pencil in the diagonals on each block, then, using a 13mm (½) wood bit, drill the central point to a depth of a few millimetres.

8. To work out the height needed for the topmost steel rods, measure the distance from floor to ceiling, subtract the full rod length, then subtract the depth of the blocks + 2cm (¾"), and saw 8 lengths of rod to the final measurement (here rounded up to 72cm (2'4")).

Step-by-step-guide

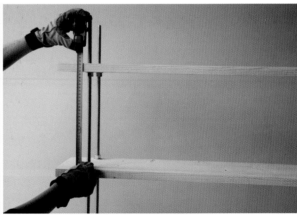

9. Fit 16 threaded rods with nuts and washers: 8 x 1m(3'3") for the bottom and 8 x 72cm(2'4") (in this example) for the top. Gently screw the rods into the blocks, taking care to avoid splitting the wood.

10. Start assembling the shelves from the bottom, beginning with the left-hand section. Position the nuts and washers for the bottom shelf by measuring its height against the bottom threaded rods.

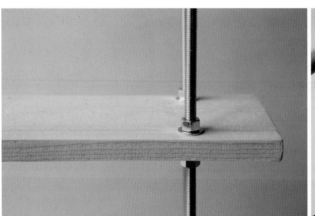

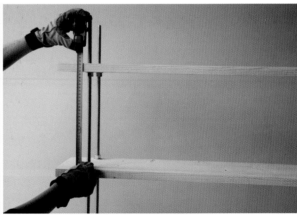

11. Thread the rods through the shelf, then add another nut and washer to each rod.

12. Continue assembling the shelves, positioning the nuts to fix their height. Repeat the process for the right-hand section, followed by the first full-length (2.4m (7'10")) shelf.

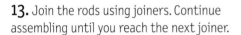

13. Join the rods using joiners. Continue assembling until you reach the next joiner.

14. Make the top section of the bookcase, working on the floor.

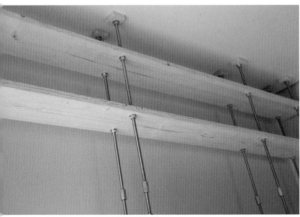

15. Fit the top section into the joiners and tighten the nuts to adjust the wooden blocks.

16. Tighten all the blocks with a spanner to ensure the bookcase fits tightly between floor and ceiling and is vertical and stable.

SPIRIT OF INDUSTRY

Seduced by the architecture of a 1920s industrial malt house, Nathalie and Frédéric set out to restore it and convert it into living space.

With architect Maureen Gâté, they have preserved the building's architectural and industrial heritage by retaining its original materials, including its brickwork and metal beam.

The same spirit also informs the staircase and library, designed in black metal and natural wood.

DESIGN:
AGENCE MGA ARCHITECTE DPLG

SPIRIT OF INDUSTRY

IN NATHALIE AND FRÉDÉRIC'S WORDS ...

'We fell in love with this disused workshop, which offered us the space we were looking for. It was a big project, with everything to do, but the spaces offered such a lot of potential. From our very first visit we could picture how it would look, even down to the position of the bookshelves! It was obvious. Then Maureen Gâté took our ideas and gave them shape. We decided to use metal to echo the original materials, and wood to add warmth to what would be the living room. The bookshelves are impressive while also remaining simple and sober in their form and materials, so they fit perfectly into this industrial setting.'

CLOSE-UP ON MATERIALS

BLACK METAL

Strong and durable, metal makes an ideal material for fittings with a contemporary aesthetic. Here the metal sections consist of hollow 4(1½") x 4cm(1½") box section. The whole structure of the bookshelves was treated against rust, then painted with black metal paint in a hammered finish.

RECONSTITUTED SOLID OAK

The shelves are made from 2cm(¾") reconstituted solid wood, a process that produces planks of large dimensions and enhanced strength. Cheaper than classic solid oak, it looks just as good.

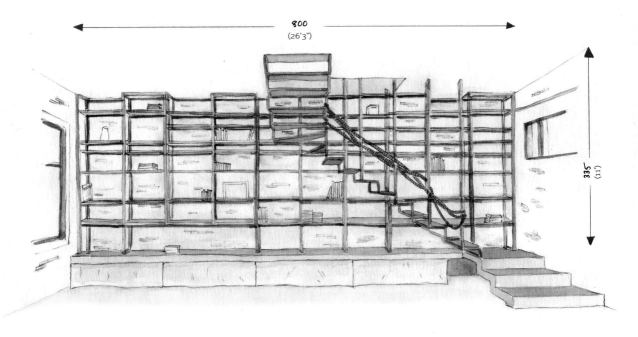

800
(26'3")

335
(11')

All measurements are given in centimetres and inches (to nearest fraction).

Construction

The architects designed a bespoke bookcase, unique and made to measure. Assembled and welded in situ by the locksmith and welder Philippe Massieu, it took nearly six weeks and 800 welds to construct. The oak shelves rest on the horizontal bars and are secured against the uprights naturally by notches.

A MULTI-FUCNTIONAL SYSTEM

While the shelves on the ground floor are filled with books and CDs, those upstairs hold boxes and filing. Here the multi-functional aspect of this system comes into its own: the bookcase serves as essential storage space for an office space slotted into a corner of the landing.

AN AIRY STAIRCASE

The owners' brief was for 'a bookcase and staircase combined'. Built in the same materials as the bookcase, the single winder stair blends into the overall decorative scheme. Suspended from the ceiling by the banisters and stripped of stringboard and risers, its airy design allows light to circulate freely and the eye to travel unobstructed.

BOOKCASE AND CD RACK COMBINED

As well as books, the shelves also hold Frédéric's impressive CD collection. Pieces of sculpture are displayed between the books and CDs, creating a decorative divider between the two and introducing a feeling of space and airiness.

Agence MGA architecte DPLG
Maureen Gâté

Maureen in 6 dates

2004: Graduates from the *Ecole Nationale Supérieure d'Architecture*, Paris Belleville.

2006: Sets up her own architectural practice.

2008: Appoints her first employee, Maximilien Massieu.

2011: Builds her first new house.

2012: Enlarges the practice.

'As a child I'd spend all my time playing with construction toys. And as a teenager I used to draw plans of the sets of television series. By the time I was sixteen, I knew I wanted to be an architect.' It's a passion that has stayed with her. After qualifying, she practised with the Lobjoy & Bouvier agency before setting up her own practice in 2006. Her work is inspired above all by her experiences on site, 'creating designs for people who want to use space.'

What are your tips for making a bookcase?

Books have a place in every room of the house, from the sitting room to the bedroom. It's important to define the type of space you are looking for, as the spot you choose will dictate the scale and style of your bookshelves. Take measurements and work out the room's individual qualities, its advantages and disadvantages.

Another determining factor will be the number and type of books you need to display. Do you have 100, 500 or 2000? Are they paperbacks or large art books? Take time to work out your needs. These, in combination with the space you have available, will enable you to work out the most appropriate arrangement.

Then you need to work out what you want in terms of a piece of furniture. Do you want something that is primarily decorative and aesthetic? Or do you want something functional, in which the aesthetic value is created by the books and other objects you want to display? These are two complementary functions, and you need to work out the balance that will suit you.

Finally, before you start work on your bookshelves, make sketches of your ideas.

Tell us some of your favourite books.

Pride and Prejudice by Jane Austen.
The Hours by Michael Cunningham.
La Nuit des Temps by René Barjavel
(English Edition: *The Ice People*, translated by C.L.Markham).

Agence MGA architecte DPLG

1 bis, rue Albert-Ier,
92600 Asnières-sur-Seine, France
Tel: +33 (0)1 55 02 30 06

agence@mga-architectes.com
www.mga-architectes.com

Spirit of Industry (p. 56)

BILLY feat. MONDRIAN

An iconic popular design meets a pioneer of abstraction. When the cult Ikea bookcase takes inspiration from the paintings of Piet Mondrian, the bookcase becomes a tableau vivant. The painter's *Composition* series and Ikea's 'Billy' bookcase make a perfect match.

Play with the colours and volumes to give free rein to your own artistic vision.

DESIGN:
JEAN-MARIE REYMOND

BILLY feat. MONDRIAN

TOOLBOX

Tools	Materials
▪ Screwdriver	▪ 2 white 'Billy' bookcases from Ikea
▪ Jigsaw	*80(2'7½") x 28(2") x 202cm(6'7½")*
▪ Stanley knife	▪ 1 white 'Billy' bookcase from Ikea
▪ Hammer	*40(1'3") x 28(2") x 202cm(6'7½")*
▪ Spatula	▪ Single-thread multi-purpose wood screws
▪ 120-grit sandpaper	▪ Nails
▪ Screw gun (wood bit + countersink bit)	▪ Filler (white)
▪ Sash (round) paintbrush	▪ 5 *19mm(¾")* x *5m(16'4")* lengths black melamine-coated adhesive tape
▪ Small paint roller	▪ Undercoat
	▪ Acrylic paint: red, yellow, blue and black

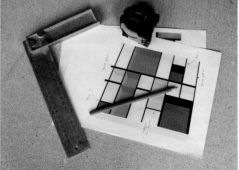

Telling details: Self-coloured ornaments add an original decorative note, while the height of the shelves can be adjusted to accommodate a variety of objects.

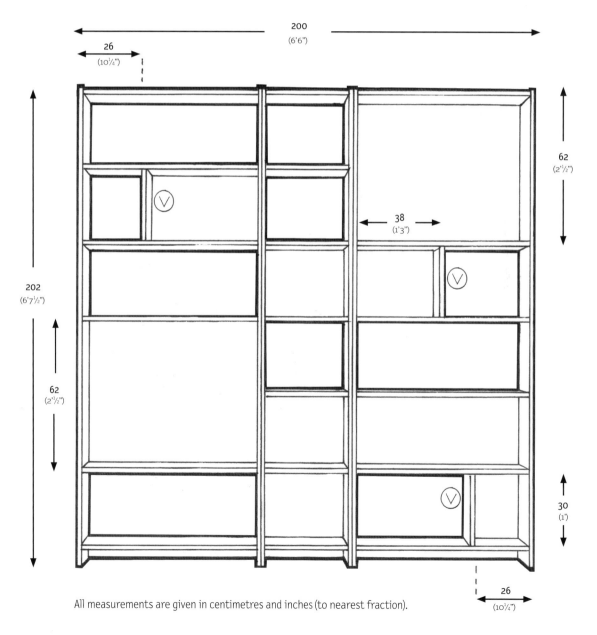

200
(6'6")

26
(10¼")

62
(2'½")

38
(1'3")

202
(6'7½")

62
(2'½")

30
(1')

26
(10¼")

All measurements are given in centimetres and inches (to nearest fraction).

Step-by-step-guide

1.Assemble the three bookcases according to the instructions, but without their backs.

2. Position the shelves as in the diagram.

3. To make the three vertical dividers ('V' on the diagram), take the extra shelves and use a fine blade to cut off the notched edges.

4. Mark the distance between the two shelves (here 30cm (1')), then cut along the mark to make the divider.

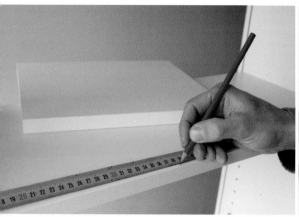

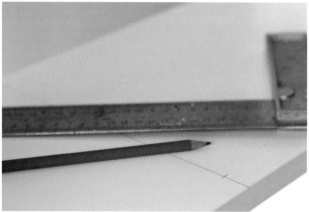

5. Mark the position of the divider on the shelves above and below.

6. Then mark the positions of the screws.

7. Pre-drill pilot holes in the shelves.

8. Use the countersink bit to countersink the screw holes.

Step-by-step-guide

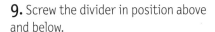

9. Screw the divider in position above and below.

10. To conceal the screws, use a spatula to fill the screw holes with filler, smoothing off any surplus. When dry, sand lightly with 120-grit sandpaper.

11. Attach the backs of the bookcases, then draw round the interiors of the sections to be painted in a colour.

12. Draw a second line 1cm (½") outside the first one (the margin needed to nail the back to the bookcase), then cut out with a jigsaw. Tip: To save time, write the final colour in each section.

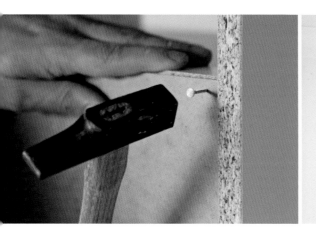

13. Nail on the back sections to be painted.

14. To make them more stable, screw the three bookcases together, using the readymade screw holes.

15. Paint the coloured sections with an undercoat for laminated surfaces to ensure better adhesion for the paint. Then apply two coats of the coloured paints.

16. Position the adhesive tape along the front edges of the shelves and uprights and cut with a Stanley knife. As the tape will be wider than the shelf edges, take care to position it flush with the top edge and overlapping the bottom edge. This will avoid it catching when you take books out. Alternatively, you can paint the edges.

Body and Soul!
Cook & Book/Brussels

Set in the Wolubilis complex at Woluwé-Saint-Lambert, Cook & Book combines books and restaurants in premises covering 1500 square metres (16,000 sq.ft.) This unique space encompasses nine literary worlds on different themes, from graphic novels to literary fiction, via cookery and English-language publications, each with its own café tables to tempt readers to linger for a coffee or a snack.

THE DECORATIONS ARE CAREFULLY DESIGNED TO DEFINE EACH DIFFERENT WORLD. IN THE TRAVEL SECTION, A RETRO AMERICAN AIRSTREAM CARAVAN TAKES PRIDE OF PLACE.

THE CHILDREN'S SECTION - ALL EYE-POPPING PRIMARY COLOURS AND A POP ART-INSPIRED DÉCOR - IS OVERFLOWING WITH CHILDREN'S BOOKS AND TOYS.

Opened by Déborah Drion and Cédric Legein in 2006, Cook & Book is a unique concept inspired by their desire to 'bring books to life'. A true cultural hub, it hosts exhibitions, book signings and concerts throughout the year.

Cook & Book
1, place du Temps-Libre
1200 Woluwé-Saint-Lambert, Brussels, Belgium
Tel: +32 (0)2 761 26 00
www.cookandbook.com

1. In the literary fiction section, 800 volumes are suspended from the ceiling.
2. 'Cucina', dedicated to cookery books and gastronomy, channels the looks of an Italian trattoria.

CHARLOTTE UP

Simple and economic to make, *Charlotte Up* uses wooden pallets to play on notions of verticality that echo the city skyline. The flexibility of the design makes it adaptable to spaces of any size or shape, according to your needs.

DESIGN: LES M&M DESIGNERS
CONSTRUCTION: AURÉLIE DROUET

TOOLBOX

Tools

- Handsaw
- Jigsaw
- Hacksaw
- Screw gun
- Eccentric drill + sanding block
- Clamps
- Spanner and socket
- Metal file
- Paintbrushes (1 flat, long reach with angled head; 1 round; 1 flat)

Materials

- 2 106 (3'6") x 106cm (3'6") 3-stringer pallets with overhanging deckboards
- 2 86 (2'10") x 110cm (3'7") 4-stringer reversible pallets
- ø8mm (⁵/₁₆") dowels
- Wood glue
- 32 nuts, bolts + washers ø5 (³/₁₆") x 40mm (1½")
- Coloured chalk
- Paint in the colour of your choice

Telling details: the bookcase has a distinctive stepped design, with the books adding splashes of colour.

For the cuts to make, see the guide on p.183

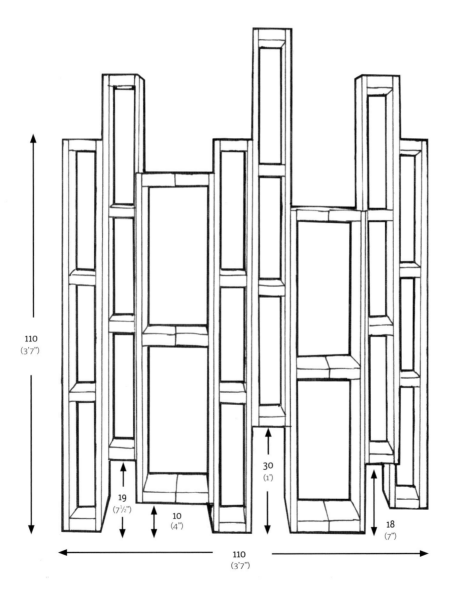

110
(3'7")

19
(7½")

10
(4")

30
(1')

18
(7")

110
(3'7")

All measurements are given in centimetres and inches (to nearest fraction).

Step-by-step-guide

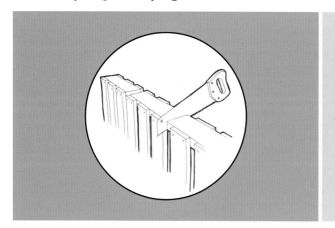

1. Saw each of the reversible pallets into 3 sections (2 with 3 boards, 1 with 2 boards), as shown on p.183.

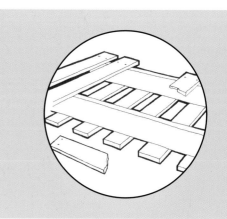

2. Remove the bottom deckboards from the pallets with overhanging boards. The pallets will be used to make the taller modules.

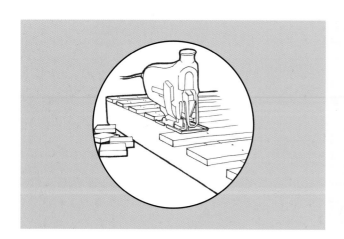

3. Saw off the overhanging sections of the top deckboards.

4. Saw both pallets into sections with 3 boards, following the guide on p.183. Discard the offcuts.

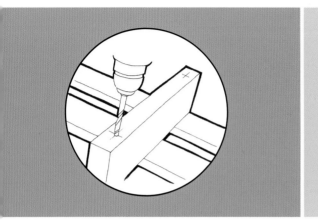

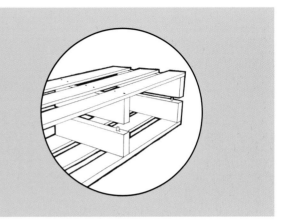

5. Each taller module is constructed from 2 sections of 3 boards, placed stringer to stringer and assembled using dowels. Using a 9mm $(^{11}/_{32})$ diameter wood drill bit for 8mm $(^{5}/_{16})$ dowels, drill 2 holes into each of the stringers of one section, then insert the dowels.

6. Cover the dowel ends liberally with coloured chalk, then position the second section precisely over the first one and press down to transfer the marks to the top section.

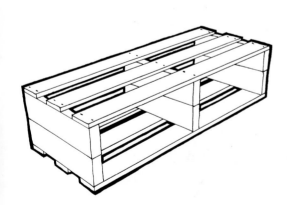

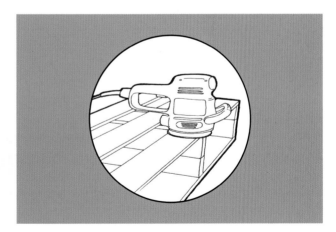

7. After drilling the stringers of the second section, check the two sections together for fit. Remove the dowels, place some wood glue in each hole, then replace the dowels to consolidate the structure.

8. Sand all the modules.

Step-by-step-guide

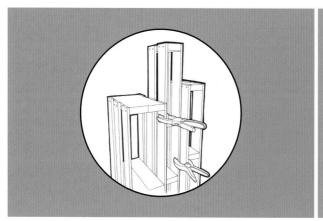

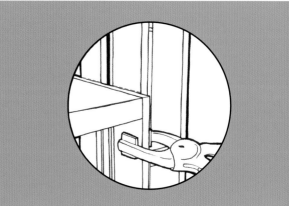

9. Position the modules side by side, playing on the different heights, then clamp them in position.

10. Mark the modules with discreet guide lines in order to make it easier to reassemble them after drilling.

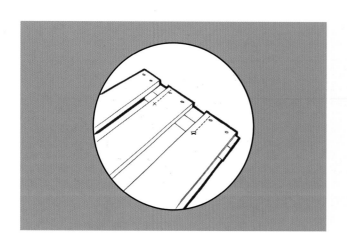

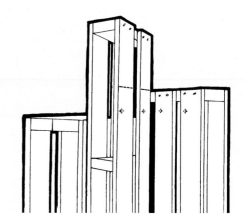

11. On the first module, mark out the positions of the bolts. Drill the holes using a bit of the same diameter as the bolts.

12. Reassemble the first and second modules and use the holes in the first module to mark the bolt positions on the second. Disassemble and drill the second module. Repeat this step on all the modules.

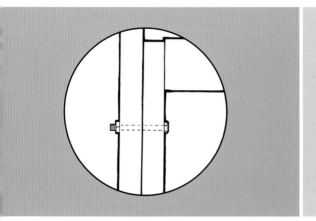 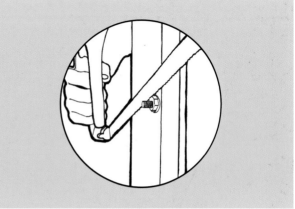

13. Screw in the bolts and washers and use a spanner and socket to tighten the bolts.

14. To protect the books from damage, saw off the excess length of the bolts beyond the nut.

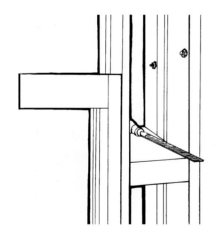 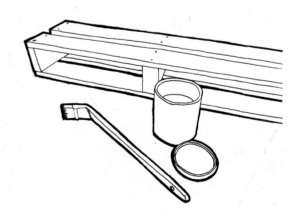

15. File the cut ends with a metal rasp.

16. Paint the inner faces, using a flat brush and a round brush to finish. A long reach brush with an angled head will make it easier to reach the central board of the 3-board modules.

M&M Designers
Martin Lévêque & Mathieu Maingourd

Martin & Mathieu in 8 dates

1980: Mathieu Maingourd is born at Rosny-sous-Bois, France, Martin Lévêque in Limoges, France.

1999: They meet as students at the ESAA in Troyes.

2002: Matheiu joins the firm of Céline and works as a designer with Hannah Norman and Nicole Stuhlman.

2005: Martin gains a postgraduate diploma in the applied arts from La Martinière, Terreaux de Lyon.

2006: Martin moves to Brussels and works with the designer Xavier Lust.

2008: Mathieu gains a postgraduate diploma from the Ecole Supérieure des Beaux-Arts in Angers.

2010: Martin works with the architect Santiago Cirugeda's Recetas Urbans practice in Seville. Mathieu launches a freelance career.

2012: Mathieu designs games in situ for a school in Senegal.

Between Nantes and Brussels, distance is no object to Martin and Mathieu, who have regular meetings to work on joint projects with a shared philosophy: artistic design, technical ingenuity and humanity lie at the heart of their creations. Music, literature, design, architecture: they draw their inspiration from their environment and daily lives to create designs that 'tell a story'.

How did you start designing bookcases?
Charlotte up was the result of an idea that we had when we designed our Charlotte shelf unit, also made from pallets, for another book in this series. Charlotte went from the horizontal to the vertical, and the compartments became ideal for storing large-format books. We used the structural qualities of the pallet to make a solid bookcase that was also so simple that anyone could make and adapt it.

What inspires your designs?
When it comes to storage units, we particularly admire Shiro Kuramata's *Slide 2*. And Tejo Remy's *Chest of Drawers*, made from salvaged drawers framed in maple and bundled together, is a unique and original critique of consumerism. When it came to *Charlotte up*, we were inspired by the *Random* bookcase by Neuland, with its simple, graphic clarity and rhythm.

What are your tips for making a bookcase?
The most important factor is stability, as when it is filled with books a bookcase is extremely heavy and potentially dangerous. The structure needs to be stable, and the compartments appropriate for the dimensions of books. But it is also useful to play with the modules and their arrangement, to endow a piece of furniture that tends to be imposing with a new sense of lightness.

Tell us some of your favourite books.
Mathieu: *Replay* by Ken Grimwood.
Martin: *Oro* by Cizia Zykë (translated into English by Stanley Hochman).

Martin Lévêque
44, rue Eeckelaers - 1210 Brusses, Belgium
Tel: +32 (0)4 85 78 55 19
martinlvqe@gmail.com/www.be.net/martinleveque

Mathieu Maingourd
massiouxx@gmail.com/www.be.net/math_ology

Charlotte Up (p. 74)

LA FABRIQUE

La Fabrique is simplicity itself, with concrete blocks and wooden planks forming the basis of a bookcase of clean lines and pared-back restraint.

The monochrome understatement of this black-and-white version only adds to the elegance of both the design and the materials.

DESIGN:
AURÉLIE DROUET

LA FABRIQUE

TOOLBOX

Tools

- Jigsaw
- Sanding block
- Coarse-grit sandpaper
- Fine round paintbrush
- Paint roller
- Small long-pile masonry roller

Materials

- 15 concrete *20cm(8")* square cube blocks
- 3 *1.5m(4'11")* pine shelves, *2.5(1") x 80cm(2'7½")*
- Matt black paint
- White acrylic paint
- Clear matt varnish

Telling details: The combination of textured and smooth finishes and the black-and-white palette add a note of understated elegance.

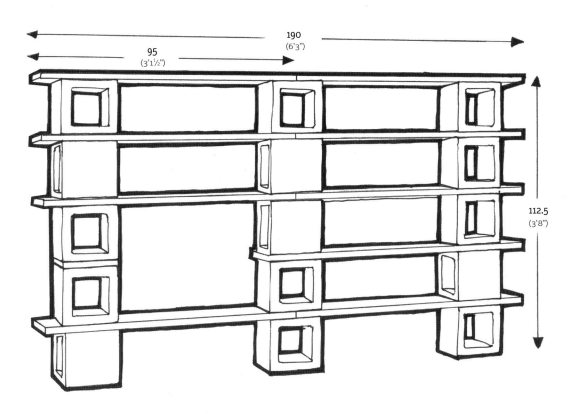

All measurements are given in centimetres and inches (to nearest fraction).

Step-by-step-guide

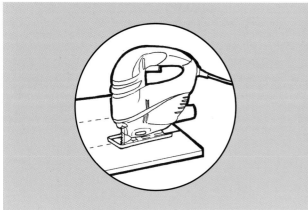

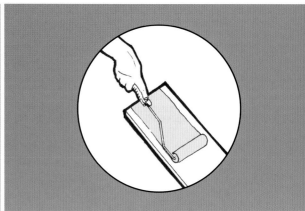

1. Saw the pine boards as follows:
- 8 planks measuring 25 (9¾") x 95cm (3'1½")
- 1 plank measuring 25 (9¾") x 107cm (3' 6')
- 1 square measuring 20 (8") x 20cm (8")

2. Paint the planks with matt black paint. When they are dry, apply two coats of clear matt varnish.

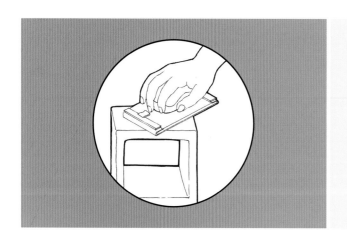

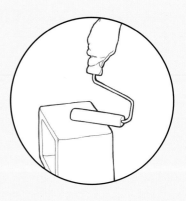

3. Use coarse-grit sandpaper to smooth the roughness of the concrete cubes, taking particular care over the edges.

4. Paint the cubes with two layers of paint. Use a small long-pile masonry roller to cover the unevenness of the surface. Paint the wood square white.

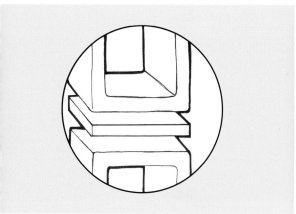

5. Position the wood square between two of the concrete cubes as shown. This will make the double-height shelf.

6. Position the concrete uprights, alternating the open and closed sides facing outwards.

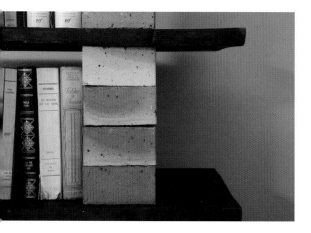

7. As a variation on the same theme, bricks can be combined with varnished wood to create a similarly authentic look.

IN THE RAW

With its structure composed of concrete reinforcing rods and MDF boards, the bookcase in Justine and Gabin's hall creates a sense of airy lightness.

Discreetly tucked into a passageway, it fills a space that would otherwise be lost. Clean lines and raw materials combine to lend it an air of distinction.

DESIGN:
BULLE CRÉA CONCEPT

IN THE RAW

IN JUSTINE AND GABIN'S WORDS ...

'We had renovated the house and completely altered the internal layout.
We spent ages looking for a bookcase to stand against the wall in the spacious hall,
a passageway between the first floor, our bedroom and the living room. It had to be shallow,
in order not to get in the way, and also light, so as not to impinge on the space visually
between the stairs and the bedroom door.

And then there was the question of budget. We liked the design suggested by Bulle Créa
Concept immediately. Both the design of the bookcase and its materials answered our
needs perfectly. And now the whole family has their own shelf space!'

CLOSE-UP ON MATERIALS

CONCRETE REINFORCING RODS

Concrete reinforcing rods are made
of steel, can be smooth or notched,
and come in a range of diameters.
For maximum stability, here 20mm
(¾") rods were used for the uprights
and 16mm (⅝") for the horizontal
shelf supports.

MDF

MDF (Medium-density fibreboard) is
made by combining wood fibres with
wax and a synthetic resin binder.
Its looks, low cost and ease of use
make it a popular choice for furniture.
This bookcase uses untreated
15mm (½") boards.

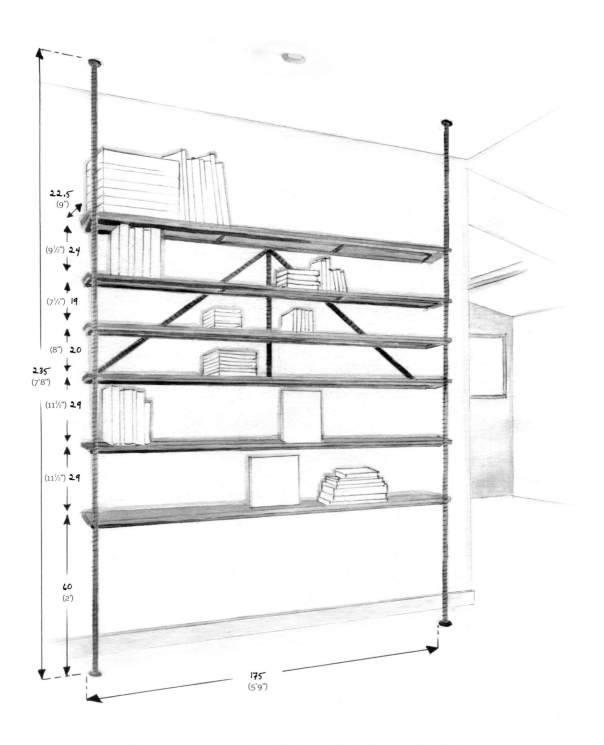

22.5
(9")

(9½") 24

(7½") 19

(8") 20

235
(7'8")

(11½") 29

(11½") 29

60
(2')

175
(5'9")

All measurements are given in centimetres and inches (to nearest fraction).

Construction

The bookcase structure consists of concrete reinforcing rods, cut and soldered together to create a bespoke shelving system. To ensure that the 240cm (7'10")-long boards do not bend under the weight of the books, the horizontal bars are reinforced by cross-struts attached to the wall. The shelves are designed to fill the full height of the wall, with the lowest one reserved for the youngest members of the family.

CALCULATING SHELF HEIGHTS

Shelves may be uniform in height, or they may vary according to the size of the books or other objects to be displayed on them. It is a good idea to make a sketch in advance in order to work out the best measurements for you. Here there are shelves of different heights for large-format books, paperbacks and CDs.

PEBBLES AS BOOKENDS

To keep their books in place, Justine and Gabin opted for the cost-saving solution of using large pebbles. Heaped on top of each other, these attractive stones make an original alternative to traditional bookends that is both practical and decorative.

FIXINGS

The concrete reinforcing rods are inserted in the ceiling and rest on the floor thanks to a system of made-to-measure circular metal plates. Matching plates finish off the ceiling fixings.

WEIGHTLESS

DESIGN

An original idea for storing books: a bookshelf that really is a book. Invisible, practical and decorative, *Weightless* covers your wall with a literary flight of fancy.

Installing this system is child's play: all you need are a few old books, some brackets and a handful of screws.

DESIGN:
AURÉLIE DROUET

WEIGHTLESS

TOOLBOX

Tools

- Stanley knife
- Tape measure
- Screw gun
- Spirit level

Materials

- 18 old hardback books
- *100mm (4")* zinc-coated steel brackets *(for paperbacks)*
- *140mm (5½")* zinc-coated steel brackets *(for larger books)*
- Single-thread multi-purpose wood screws *(small and medium)*
- Screws and rawlplugs appropriate for your wall
- Extra-strength adhesive

Telling details: The construction process could hardly be simpler, while the finished effect—
with book piles hiding the brackets—is gravity-defying.

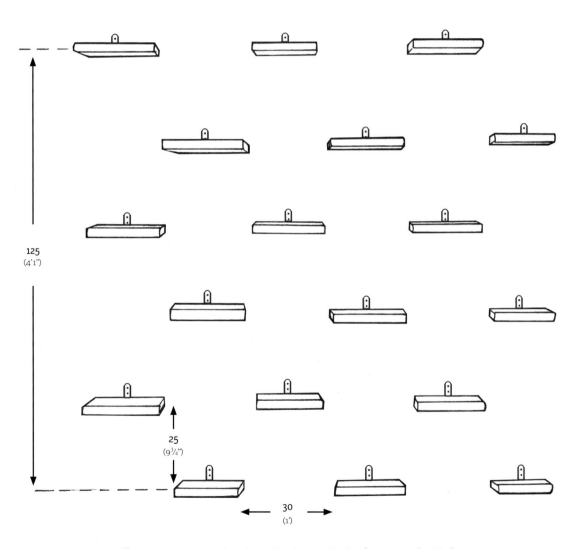

125
(4'1")

25
(9¾")

30
(1')

All measurements are given in centimetres and inches (to nearest fraction).

Step-by-step-guide

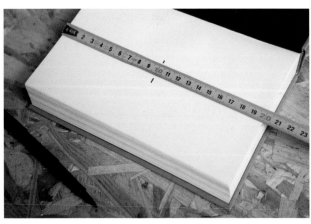

1. Take one of your old books and mark the centre of the last page.

2. Position a bracket on the page, using the screw holes to help you find the centre, then draw round it.

3. Using a Stanley knife, cut out the shape of the bracket, making the hole slightly deeper than the bracket itself so that the cover will shut flat.

4. Turn the book the right way up. Insert the bracket with the vertical side facing upwards. Cut a notch in the front cover to accommodate the thickness of the bracket and allow the book to sit flush against the wall.

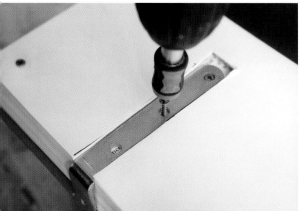

5. Turn the book face down again and screw on the bracket. Use your hand to hold the pages in place, and use small screws to screw the pages down in the corners.

6. Apply extra-strength adhesive to the last page and inside back cover. Close the book and weight it down to ensure good adhesion. Leave to dry for 12 to 24 hours.

7. Fix the book to the wall using appropriate screws and rawlplugs. Position it initially with a single screw, use a spirit level to check that it is horizontal, then insert the rest of the screws.

8. If you are using a large-format book as a shelf, use two 140mm (5¹/₂") brackets.

Literary Encounter
Shakespeare and Company/Paris

Shakespeare and Company is an independent bookshop in Paris's Left Bank, specializing in English-language books. The spiritual heir to the first Shakespeare and Company bookshop, founded by Sylvia Beach in 1919 and closed at the beginning of the Occupation, in 1940, it has become an institution celebrated worldwide. Henry Miller described it as a 'wonderland of books'.

WRITERS HAVE BEEN ABLE TO STAY IN THE BOOKSHOP SINCE THE 1950S, COMING HERE TO SEEK INSPIRATION FOR A FEW NIGHTS OR MONTHS AT A TIME.

THE PHILOSOPHY OF GEORGE WHITMAN, FOUNDER OF THE SECOND SHOP, IS INSCRIBED ABOVE A DOOR: 'BE NOT INHOSPITABLE TO STRANGERS LEST THEY BE ANGELS IN DISGUISE.'

Shakespeare and Company was founded in 1951 by George Whitman (1913–2011), and since 2005 has been run by his daughter Sylvia Beach Whitman. It hosts numerous cultural events, including author events, poetry readings, a book festival and a literary prize.

Shakespeare and Company
37, rue de la Bûcherie - 5005 Paris, France
Tel: +33 (0)1 43 25 40 93
news@shakespeareandcompany.com
www.shakespeareandcompany.com

1

2

1. Bookshop, second-hand bookstore and reading library, Shakespeare and Company is lined with books on every surface.

2. Sylvia Beach Whitman.

ANNA

One bookcase in two different versions: one moving around on castors,
the other revolving on the pedestal of an old stool.

With its unusual geometry, *Anna* offers a reversible storage solution that is ideal for
small spaces. The wheeled version, meanwhile, can trundle into any corner according
to your whim: a witty combination of style and function.

DESIGN:
JEAN-MARIE REYMOND

ANNA

TOOLBOX

Tools

- Handsaw
- Jigsaw
- Screw gun *(wood bit + countersink bit)*
- Sanding block
- Rasp
- Stanley knife
- Steel wool
- Sponge
- Spatula
- Paint roller
- Sash and flat paintbrushes

Materials

- 3 2m(6'6") pine boards *18(¾") x 500mm(1'8")*
- *7mm(¼")* bendy ply *1.22(4'1") x 2.5m(8'2")*
- 6 2m(6'6") battens *20(¾") x 20mm(¾")*
- 1 revolving bar stool, ideally old
- 4 castors
- 4 countersunk socket screws *ø5(¹³⁄₆₄) x 30mm(1¼")*
- Single-thread multi-purpose wood screws
- Filler
- Paint (2 colours) and clear varnish
- Clear varnish for metal

Telling details: Flexible, functional and practical, a revolving modular storage unit in the tradition of Anna Castelli Ferrieri's classic *Componibili* design of 1968.

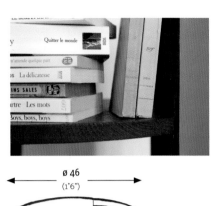

ø 46
(1'6")

1.8
(¾")

20
(8")

1.8
(¾")

40
(1'3")

97.2
(3'2")

1.8
(¾")

30
(1')

1.8
(¾")

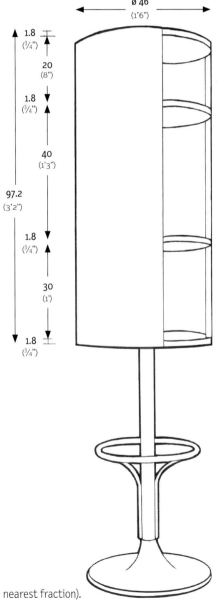

ø 46
(1'6")

1.8
(¾")

20
(8")

1.8
(¾")

40
(1'3")

119
(3'10¾")

1.8
(¾")

30
(1')

1.8
(¾")

20
(8")

1.8
(¾")

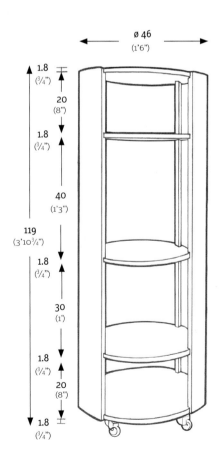

All measurements are given in centimetres and inches (to nearest fraction).

Step-by-step-guide

1. For the taller 'stool' module, use the base of the stool as a template and trace the 4 circular sections on the wooden boards. Saw along the lines, then sand the edges. For the shorter 'wheeled' version, use any circular object of the desired diameter as your template.

2. Place the 4 circular sections on top of one another, the mark out the four quarters of the circle on the top one. Extend the marks down the sides of all 4 sections as a guide for positioning the side struts.

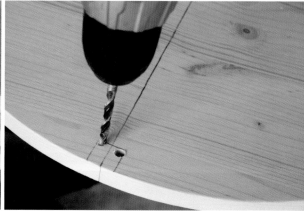

3. Take a short piece of 20 (¾") x 20mm (¾") batten, place it on each mark in turn and draw round it.

4. To saw the inner edge of each notch, just inside your guide line in each corner, drill a hole that is slightly larger in diameter than the blade of your jigsaw.

5. Saw out each notch, starting with the sides and finishing by joining the holes on the inner edge.

6. Position one of the side struts to check for fit.

7. If the side strut does not lie completely flush, deepen the notch slightly using a rasp.

8. Saw the battens to obtain 4 lengths of 97.2cm (3'2¼"). Mark out the positions of the circular sections as given on the diagram (or according to the desired shelf heights), taking care to mark the correct depth for the circular sections (here 1.8cm (¾")).

Step-by-step-guide

9. Pre-drill and countersink the centre of each of the guide marks on the side struts.

10. Using the drill holes in the side strut as a guide, pre-drill pilot holes in the circular sections to avoid the wood splitting. Screw the side struts to the circular sections.

11. To calculate the width of the bendy ply, use a length of string or cord to measure the distance between two side struts. Measure this against a ruler and add a 4cm (1½") margin.

12. Mark this measurement on the plywood, then cut it was a Stanley knife. Keep the full length of the panel as this will be adjusted later.

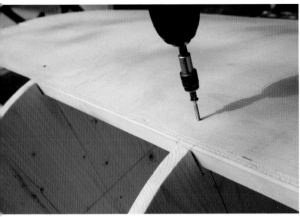

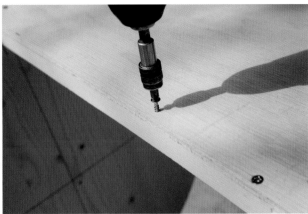

13. Screw the plywood to the edge of the circular sections in several places.

14. Screw the plywood to both side struts along their full length.

15. Use the jigsaw to saw off the surplus length.

16. Use a Stanley knife to cut off the surplus width, cutting flush with the side struts.

Step-by-step-guide

17. Apply filler to the joints and screw heads with a spatula, then leave to dry.

18. Sand the filler down using fine-grit sandpaper.

19. Apply two coats of the coloured paint of your choice, then apply a coat of varnish. Here *Anna* is painted in two shades of grey, lighter outside and darker inside. To make the shorter module, repeat all these steps.

20. To prepare the old bar stool (or a new one if you prefer), rub down the whole of the pedestal with steel wool (but not too vigorously, as you want to keep the rusty look). Dust off with a handbrush then rinse with clean water. Leave to dry.

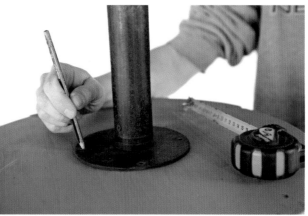

21. Apply two coats of varnish. Wait until this is completely dry before fitting the module on top.

22. To attach the pedestal, place it in the centre of the module and use a pencil to draw through the screw holes, then drill the holes.

23. Attach the pedestal using countersunk socket screws.

24. For the wheeled version, position 4 castors under the side struts and screw them in place.

RECTO-VERSO

INSPIRATION

One of Mathieu's prime concerns in giving his 60-square-metre (646 sq.ft.) flat a makeover was finding space for his impressive collection of graphic novels and comics, a passion since childhood. The challenge for the h2o architectural practice was to design a storage and display system for his books, masks and other objects.

Their solution is an open-plan space that plays on the idea of areas of activity, presided over by a 'totem-bookcase'.

DESIGN:
h2o architectes

RECTO-VERSO

'The apartment was old, insalubrious and far too divided up. I wanted to rethink its 60 square metres (646 sq.ft.) in a way that would offer a storage system for my graphic novels. I also wanted to find a way of concealing the television and the office area.

The architects have created a perfect solution: an open-plan space with a bespoke system containing numerous different built-in storage spaces. Their starting point was calculating how many metres of graphic novels and comics I needed to accommodate, and from this there followed the arrangement of niches in the central bookcase and other furniture, all designed along geometric lines.'

CLOSE-UP ON MATERIALS

BENDY PLY

Bendy ply consists of panels of 3 to 5 veneers, often of exotic woods, which can be bent along the grain of the wood to give a wide range of curving shapes.

Light, flexible and easy to work with, bendy ply is used extensively in furniture and interior design. Here the curved furniture is made with bendy ply using 3 7mm (¼") veneers.

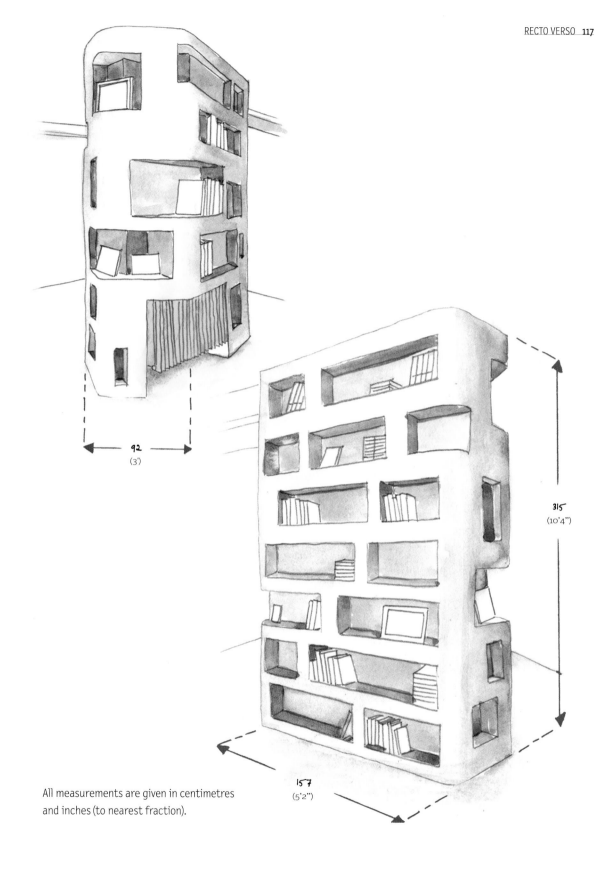

92
(3')

315
(10'4")

157
(5'2")

All measurements are given in centimetres
and inches (to nearest fraction).

Construction

The smooth surfaces and simple geometry of the design have been created in plasterboard. The curved items are made from bendy ply, sanded and primed before being painted. The bespoke furniture contains false bottoms, drawers and foldaway work surfaces. For the architects, 'the recto always contains its own counter-shape, its own verso; the reverse side of any décor can be revealed to make room for new uses.'

THE TOTEM

The h2o practice's response to the constraints imposed by a load-bearing wall and existing chimney flue was to create a central feature, around which different areas of activity were articulated. The 'totem', which divides the dining area from the sitting area, holds Mathieu's graphic novels and figurines: a bookcase that both structures and optimizes the space.

COLOURING CODING

Niches of different shapes and sizes are a feature of the apartment, colour-coded according to their function: green for the kitchen and bathroom, orange for the office area and grey for books. Grey was chosen as a neutral shade to act as a foil to the vivid colours of the graphic novels and comics.

DISCREET STORAGE

The wall in the sitting/living area contains a combination of open and closed storage spaces, forming a graphic composition that is also practical. The television is concealed behind built-in bookshelves.

h2o architectes
Charlotte Hubert, Jean-Jacques Hubert & Antoine Santiard

h2o in 6 dates

1999: Charlotte graduates from the Ecole Nationale Supérieure d'Architecture, Paris-Belleville (followed by the Ecole de Chaillot in 2004). Jean-Jacques graduates from the Ecole Nationale Supérieure d'Architecture, Nantes.

2001: Antoine graduates from the Ecole Polytechnique, Lausanne.

2005: They set up the h2o architectural practice.

2008: h2o wins the Nouveaux Albums prize for young architects, awarded by the French Ministry of Culture and Communication.

2009: Wallpaper magazine includes h2o in its list of the 30 best young international architectural practices.

2012: Their project for 20 social housing units and 3 commercial units in the eleventh arrondissement of Paris is nominated for the Le Moniteur Premier Œuvre prize.

Heritage, architecture, urban development, landscape design, furniture design: h2o is the epitome of a cross-disciplinary approach. The projects handled by the practice reflect the complementary skills of its three partners, and echo the qualities of continuity, inventiveness and consistency that form the central thread running through their philosophy. In order conceive a design and communicate it, they believe that you must 'look, understand and give'. Their strong and varied portfolio bears witness to the recognition their skills have gained.

What are your tips for making a bookcase?

A bookcase should be like a cocoon, warm and reassuring; it's not just another piece of furniture, it's much more personal. Some people really stress over how to organize their books. Everyone likes to arrange them differently, but for anyone who's not terribly organized we recommend ordering them simply by size: that way the shelves vary in height and together they create a visual harmony. Set aside spaces here and there for decorative objects or ornaments. And remember to create a solid structure, as books are heavy: use materials that won't buckle under their weight. Don't skimp on shelf space—you can never have enough.

If you decide to opt for a really tall bookcase, build in a ladder or steps to reach the top shelves. To give it a double use, make the steps or rungs deep enough to sit on. If you have art books in your library, position them face outwards to enjoy their cover artwork. You might even consider designing in a small desk to sit at as you consult them.

Tell us some of your favourite books.

Charlotte: *Philibert de l'Orme, Traités d'architecture* by Jean-Marie Pérouse de Montclos (Léonce Laget).
Jean-Jacques: *The Dice Man* by Luke Rhinehart (HarperCollins).
Antoine: *La Société du spectacle* by Guy Debord (Gallimard); translated into English by Tom Vague as *The Society of the Spectacle* (Black & Red).

h2o architectes

24, place Raoul-Fol_lereau - 75010 Paris, France
Tel.: +33 (0)9 64 00 52 81

contact@h2oarchitectes.com
www.h2oarchitectes.com

Recto-verso (p. 114)

MEREDITH

This 'book-bench' takes its inspiration from a classic piece of furniture, the meridienne. In old French, *la méridienne* was the name for a siesta; in this wooden version, *Meredith* invites readers to indulge in time out with a good book.

This multi-functional piece will happily adapt to any room in the house.

DESIGN:
JEAN-MARIE REYMOND

MEREDITH

TOOLBOX

Tools

- Jigsaw
- Rasp
- Screwdriver
- Screw gun (wood bit + countersink bit)
- Spatula
- Fine-grit sandpaper
- Eccentric sander
- Small paint roller
- Fine round paintbrush

Materials

- 4 2m(6'6") pine boards 18(¾") x 400mm(1'3")
- 5 14cm(5½") L black metal rectangular furniture legs
- Single-thread multi-purpose wood screws ø4(^{5}/$_{32}$) x 45mm(1¾")
- Filler
- Extra-strength adhesive
- Clear matt varnish
- Paint in colors of your choice
- Small clip-on reading lamp

Telling details: A bench and bookcase, two pieces of furniture in one, painted in an eye-catching combination of colours.

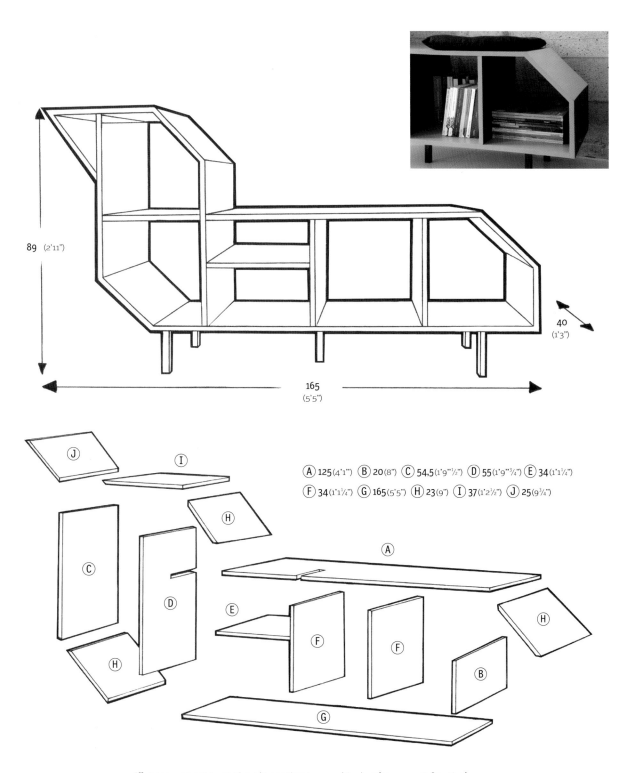

89 (2'11")

40 (1'3")

165 (5'5")

(A) 125(4'1") (B) 20(8") (C) 54.5(1'9''½") (D) 55(1'9''¾") (E) 34(1'1¼")

(F) 34(1'1¼") (G) 165(5'5") (H) 23(9") (I) 37(1'2½") (J) 25(9¾")

All measurements are given in centimetres and inches (to nearest fraction).

Step-by-step-guide

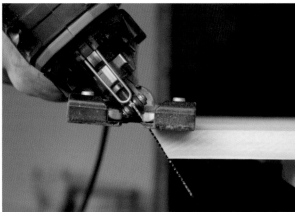

1. Prepare all the sections by sawing the boards to the dimensions shown on the diagram.

2. Chamfer the ends of sections H at 45-degree angles. Note: 23cm (9") corresponds to the length of the shorter side.

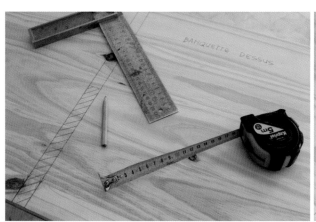

3. To assemble the seat and backrest, mark out a first notch on the seat (section A on the diagram), 34cm (1'1") from one of the ends. Make the notch 1.8cm (¾") wide (the depth of a board) and half the width, 20cm (8")

4. To saw the inner end of the notch, drill two holes slightly larger in diameter than the blade of your jigsaw against the inside of the marked line.

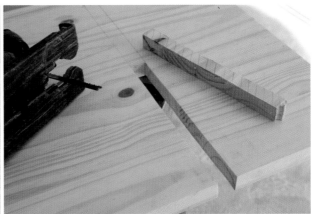

5. Saw the notch, starting with the sides and finishing by sawing between the two holes.

6. Repeat steps 3 to 5 for the notch on the backrest (section D on the diagram), positioning it 17cm (6³/₄") from the end of the board.

7. Slot together sections A and D.

8. Screw the seat and backrest firmly together. To conceal the screw heads, mark the positions on section A and countersink the holes.

Step-by-step-guide

9. Pre-drill pilot holes at a slight angle.

10. Insert the screws, also at a slight angle.

11. Mark the positions of the vertical dividers F and the positions of the screws on both the top and bottom of section A. Countersink then drill them.

12. Spread adhesive on sections F and position these under the seat, against the marks made earlier.

13. Screw sections F to section A.

14. Repeat steps 11 to 13 to assemble sections F and section G.

15. Continue to assemble all the sections: countersink, pre-drill, glue then screw.

16. To fix sections H and J, position each section against the straight-cut edge of the section to which it needs to be screwed. Mark the midpoint of the straight-cut edge, then continue this line on to sections H and J to mark the positions of the screws.

Step-by-step-guide

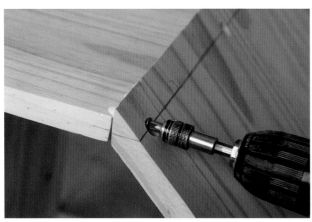

17. Countersink, pre-drill and glue sections H and J, then insert the screws.

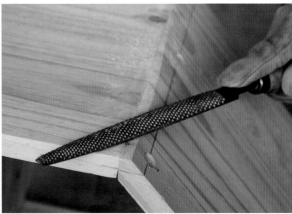

18. If the sections do not sit completely flush with one another, use a rasp to file off the excess.

19. Sand the surface to make it completely smooth.

20. Use filler to fill the screw holes and conceal the screw heads. Apply the filler with a spatula, then scrape of the excess. When dry, sand lightly using a 120-grit sandpaper.

21. Following the same process, fill the gaps between the sections.

22. Apply two coats of paint, using a small roller for the flat surfaces and a small round brush for the angles and edges. When the paint is dry, apply one or two coats of clear matt varnish for protection.

23. Screw on the legs, placing the fifth one in the centre of the book-bench.

24. A small clip-on reading lamp makes the ideal finishing touch. Clip it on wherever it suits and adjust the beam to create optimum conditions for reading.

Jean-Marie Reymond
Designer

Jean-Marie in 5 dates :

1981: Born in Saint-Nazaire.

1997: Spends a year in the United States.

2006: Graduates in interior design and architecture from the Ecole Pivaut, Nantes.

2009: Spends six months travelling in India and Nepal.

2013: Exhibits his design for the Line coat rack in the Sixth Sense exhibition at the Saint-Etienne International Design Biennale.

Initially trained in industrial design [this isn't mentioned in his key dates?], this imaginative young designer is now interested primarily in eco-design, finding inspiration in objects and their stories. Recycling and combining are the watchwords governing his approach, which he describes as 'ethical and pragmatic'. Evolving between the artistic and the artisanal, his designs are challenging and seductive in their simplicity.

How did you start designing bookcases?
My idea was to develop different types of bookcase to serve different functions – aesthetic, accessible, practical, wall-hung, freestanding, etc. – and to go in different rooms, whether sitting room, bedroom or hallway. Not forgetting that they should be easy for readers to make, without any need for particular skills or special tools.

What are the inspirations behind your designs?
I draw my inspiration from my surroundings, but my thinking often starts with asking questions. What do I want to show? What is the main purpose of the piece? What story does this bookcase tell? Then I choose the materials, draw the shape or imagine a dual function, and test it out. Meredith shows how you can combine two uses in one piece, Matéo is about recycling. Every design expresses an idea.

What are your tips for making a bookcase?
Since the primary function of a bookcase is to store books, you need to define your needs carefully. Then choose a style: classic or quirky, decorative or multi-purpose. Once you have your design, all that's left is to choose your materials and have faith in yourself!

Tell us your favourite book.
Magasin général by Régis Loisel and Jean-Louis Tripp (Casterman).

Jean-Marie Reymond

6 bis, rue Noire - 44000 Nantes, France
Tel: +33(0)2 40 48 54 96
jeanmariereymond@hotmail.com
www.behance.net/jdce

33

Left to Right: Billy *feat.* Mondrian (p. 64) ▪ Anna (p. 104) ▪ Globe Reader (p. 38) ▪ Matéo (p. 134) ▪ Meredith (p. 122)

MATÉO

DESIGN

An old stepladder and some boards are all you need to make these bookshelves.
Or you could use two wooden ladders or a metal stepladder.

Matéo offers a storage solution that is not only quick and easy to make,
but also infinitely adaptable. Play with its dimensions, colours and materials
to add a personal touch and an original note to your décor.

DESIGN:
JEAN-MARIE REYMOND

MATÉO

TOOLBOX

Tools

- Jigsaw
- Screw gun
- Mitre
- Stanley knife
- Spirit level
- Masking tape
- Small paint roller
- Flat paintbrushes, small and medium

Materials

- 1 old wooden stepladder
- 2 200 (6'6") x 1.8cm (¾") pine boards to fit the width of the stepladder (here 55cm (1'9¾"))
- 1 2m (6'6") batten 2 (¾") x 2cm (¾")
- Single-thread multi-purpose wood screws
- 1 pack white cable clips
- 1 LED self-adhesive strip kit (1.5m (4'11") LED strip with connectors and transformer)
- Paint (2 colours of your choice)
- Clear matt water-based varnish

Telling details: The old stepladder in its original splendor (left), and with its LED-lit shelves.

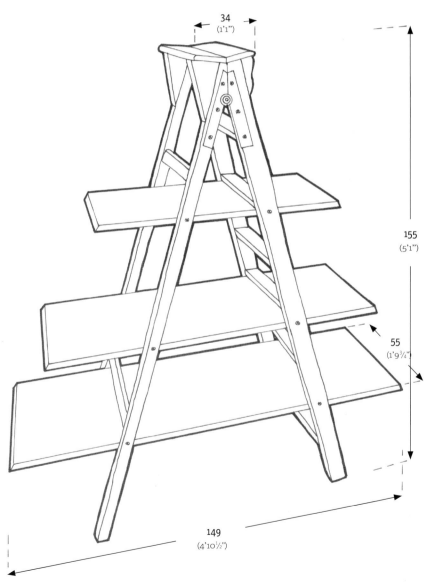

34
(1'1")

155
(5'1")

55
(1'9¾")

149
(4'10½")

All measurements are given in centimetres and inches (to nearest fraction).

Step-by-step-guide

1. Saw the boards to the desired lengths for the shelves, making a 30-degree chamfered edge. Here the lengths are graduated to follow the angle of the stepladder.

2. Using a small roller, paint the shelves in the colour of your choice.

3. Position the boards on the stepladder, taking care to ensure they are accurately centred, then pre-drill the uprights and boards at the points where they intersect. Fix the two top shelves to the underside of the steps and rest the bottom one on top of the step.

4. As reinforcement for the middle and bottom shelves, saw the batten to widths slightly shorter than the width of the boards. This will later provide the space for the LED strip.

5. Pre-drill 4 equally spaced holes in each batten.

6. Countersink the holes to conceal the screw heads.

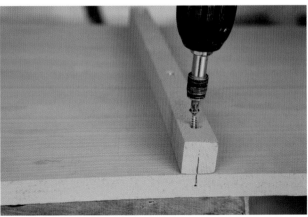

7. Paint the battens.

8. Using the pilot holes made at step 3 as your guide, screw the battens to the middle and bottom shelves.

Step-by-step-guide

9. Screw the shelves to the stepladder uprights, using a spirit level to ensure they are horizontal.

10. Screw the top and middle shelves to the underside of the steps.

11. Use masking tape to mark out lines at random. At points where they intersect, use a Stanley knife to cut the tape.

12. Paint the lines in a deeper or brighter shade than the shelves.

 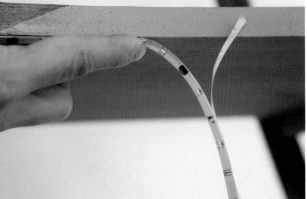

13. Use a brush to apply 2 coats of clear varnish. Leave to dry.

14. Cut the LED strip into 2 lengths for the top and middle shelf, then install it following the manufacturer's instructions.

15. Use cable clips to attach the electric cable to the length of the rear upright.

The staircase as furniture
Marc Koehler Architects/Amsterdam

To open up the volumes of a house in the Overtoom district of Amsterdam, the architect Marc Koehler has redefined the primary function of the staircase and treated it as part of the room's furnishings. In collaboration with Made-up Interior Works, it now offers an opportunity to make full use of the space in a more logical way.

THE STEPS ARE CONSTRUCTED FROM PLASTERBOARD WITH STRIPS OF FINE ANTI-SLIP TAPE ADDED.

THE OPEN STAIRCASE OFFERS POTENTIAL FOR CREATING GENEROUS SHELF SPACE.

After studying engineering, urban planning and architecture and working with Achitekten Cie, Marc Koehler set up his own practice in 2005. His built projects, teaching and research have enabled him to develop an approach to design and architecture that combines practice with theory.

Marc Koehler Architects
Keizersgracht 126 - 1015 cw Amsterdam, Holland
Tel: +31 (0)20 575 5508
office@marckoehler.nl/www.marckoehler.nl

The staircase structures the space while also transforming into an imposing bookcase.

BOX-FRESH BOOKS

Plastic trays of the kind used by garden centres, plant nurseries and market stall-holders here find a novel new life inside the house.

Available second-hand online, they can also be sourced direct from markets and garden centres.

Box-fresh Books offers an ingenious, low-cost approach to building a quirky bespoke bookcase.

DESIGN:
AURÉLIE DROUET

BOX-FRESH BOOKS

TOOLBOX	
Tools	**Materials**
▪ Bowl and sponge	▪ 18 black plastic trays, *15cm(6")D x 30cm(1')W x 40cm(1'3")L*
▪ Cloth	▪ 1 pack black plastic cable ties
▪ Jigsaw	▪ Small nails
▪ Screw gun	▪ Screws, washers and rawlplugs suitable for your wall
▪ Hammer	▪ Plasterboard offcuts
▪ Adjustable spanner	▪ Extra-strength adhesive
▪ Pincers	▪ Paint in the colour of your choice
▪ Small paint roller	
▪ Fine round paintbrush	

Telling details: Plasterboard niches add lightness and variety to this textbook
exercise in imaginative recycling.

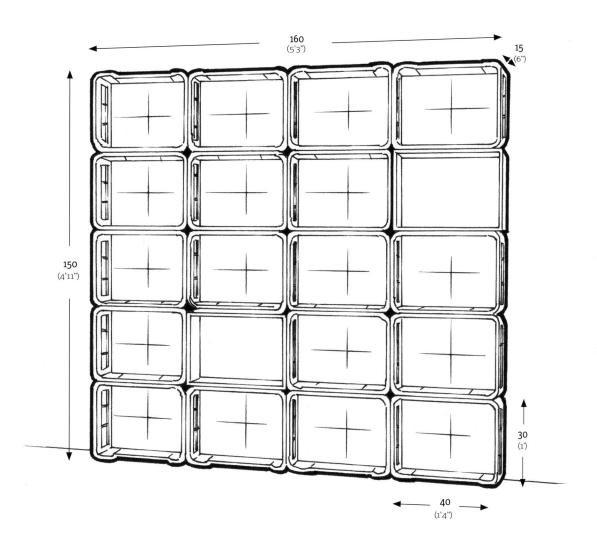

All measurements are given in centimetres and inches (to nearest fraction).

Step-by-step-guide

1. Wash the trays with soapy water and wipe them dry.

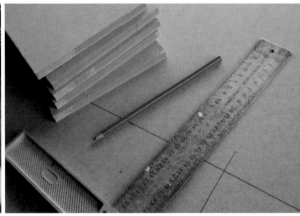

2. To make the niches, cut 8 pieces of plasterboard, 4 15(6") x 39cm(1'3") and 4 15(6") x 29cm(11^{1}/$_{2}$").

3. Glue the plasterboard niches together, then nail them.

4. Apply two coats of paint to the niches.

5. As you build your bookcase, secure the trays to each other with cable ties, using an adjustable wrench to tighten them.

6. After tightening, use pincers to cut off the excess.

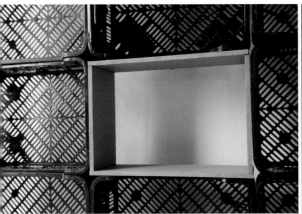 

7. Slot in your niches as you go.

8. To ensure the stability of the bookcase, fix some of the trays to the wall, using the appropriate screws and rawlplugs for your wall.

GRAPHIC DESIGN

When they converted their apartment into a duplex, Pélagie and Gauthier called on the expertise of Atelier Premier Etage to make full use of every square centimetre.

The addition of a double-sided partition and a staircase offered opportunities for creating bookshelves and other storage areas.

From the contrasting materials to the design of the compartments, this graphic design adds a distinctively individual and stylish note to the apartment.

DESIGN:
ATELIER PREMIER ÉTAGE

GRAPHIC DESIGN

IN PÉLAGIE AND GAUTHIER'S WORDS ...

'To coincide with the baby arriving, we decided that we wanted to convert the attic space in order to enlarge the apartment. What was so interesting was all the different solutions suggested by the interior designers, which went much further than our basic ideas.

The stairs are no longer lost space; instead they are a means of gaining space. And the addition of the double-sided partition meant that we could get rid of some of our furniture and create not only a bookcase but also storage space in the bedroom. Now both rooms are more spacious.'

CLOSE-UP ON MATERIALS

BATIPIN

Batipin is an environmentally friendly plywood made from maritime pine, with a pronounced grain that adds an extra dimension. This aesthetic quality, combined with its solidity and ease of use, makes it an ideal material for use in interior design.

COLOURED MDF

MDF (medium density fibreboard) is made from wood fibres mixed with wax and glue. In coloured MDF, the wood fibres are mixed with the pigments before the board is pressed, so ensuring an even colour throughout the board. Coloured MDF can be sanded and sawn like ordinary MDF, and can be finished with a coat of clear varnish or lacquer.

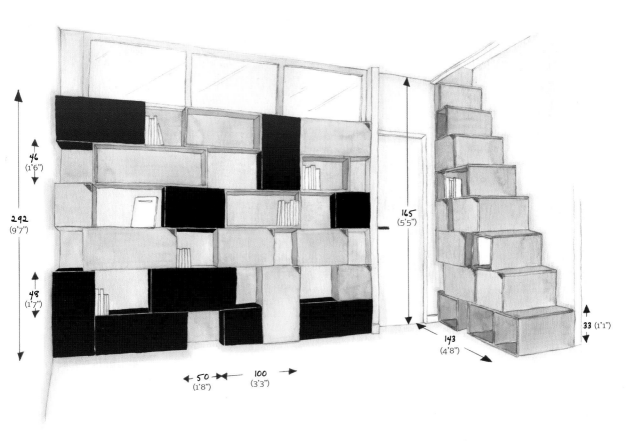

46
(1'6")

292
(9'7")

48
(1'7")

165
(5'5")

33 (1'1")

143
(4'8")

50
(1'8")

100
(3'3")

All measurements are given in centimetres and inches (to nearest fraction).

Construction

The partition and staircase are made up of storage compartments of varying sizes, with or without doors to respond to different needs. In their combination of Batipin with coloured MDF, the architects have played on the contrasts between the two materials: the rich grain and warm blond shades of the Batipin on the one hand, and on the other the cool, even, mineral colour and texture of the MDF.

A NEAT SOLUTION

With a little imagination, the space beneath the stairs can easily be put to good use. Here the staircase is formed by storage cases, with shelves taking up the full width of the space.

A DOUBLE-SIDED PARTITION

The partition combines open shelves with closed cupboard space. On the living room side it is chiefly a bookcase. On the bedroom side, meanwhile, it becomes a clothes storage solution, with precedence given to closed cupboard spaces. The interlocking design of the compartments creates a striking effect.

STRUCTURED FAÇADES

To retain the pared back feel of the design, the designers have avoided the use of door handles, preferring to simply shave a corner off the doors, so creating a structured finish to the overall effect.

Atelier Premier Etage
Claire Escalon & Nicolas Lanno

Claire & Nicolas in 6 dates

1994: Nicolas graduates in Design from the Ecole Supérieure d'Art et de Design, Saint-Etienne.

1996: Claire graduates in Design from the Ecole Supérieure d'Art et de Design, Saint-Etienne.

1998: Creation of Appartement D, a design house selling the work of young designers through a mail-order catalogue.

2003: Claire sets up the interior design practice Atelier Premier Etage.

2009: Claire and Nicolas go into partnership.

2010: Creation of Nicolas Lanno Design Paris, selling designer furniture, lights and household items.

Claire and Nicolas both had separate careers as interior designers for a few years before joining forces as Atelier Premier Etage. They also pooled their constantly evolving vision and skills, inspired by art in all its forms, in the creation of Nicolas Lanno Design Paris, for which Nicolas designed the furniture and other items under Claire's art direction.

What are your tips for making a bookcase?

Depending on the sort of arrangement you're looking for, don't hesitate to call in an interior designer – especially for a bespoke solution. It's essential to integrate the bookcase into the rest of the interior design. You have to find the right place for it – whether in a corner or in a passage, say – and make full use of its potential, for example using the full height of a room with floor-to-ceiling shelves.

Set up rhythms, with breaks in the form of dividers or varying depths. This creates space for books of different sizes and makes it easier to reach them. Try to play on busy and uncluttered spaces by leaving some sections of the shelves empty.

A bookcase is for life: you don't change a bookcase the way you might give in to the temptation of a new chair or vase. It's an investment, so you need to set aside a realistic budget to design and build it.

Tell us some of your favourite books.

Claire: *What I Loved* by Siri Hustvedt (Sceptre)

Nicolas: *Une Vie de creation* by Charlotte Perriand (Odile Jacob); translated into English as *A Life of Creation* (Monacelli Press).

Atelier Premier Etage

3, rue Victor-Letalle - 75020 Paris, France
Tel.: +33 (0)6 03 69 53 94

claire.escalonlanno@gmail.com
www.premieretage.com/www.nicolaslanno.com

CRATE CREATION

Wooden crates — once used to transport wine, apples and other goods — are now highly prized for the possibilities they offer for stylish recycled storage solutions.

These vintage crates are ideal for creating large and versatile bookcases. Snap up any you see at flea markets and online, but be prepared to be patient as they are becoming increasingly hard to find.

The construction is finished off with a professionally made surround of melamine-coated poplar boards.

DESIGN:
GENÈVE & NICOLAS

CRATE CREATION

TOOLBOX

Tools

- Bowl and sponge
- Soda crystals (washing soda)
- Screw gun
- Jigsaw

Materials

- Vintage wooden crates *(here 21 crates, 43cm (1'5") W x 61cm (2') L x 16 (7¾"), 20(8") or 22cm (8¾") D)*
- 1 panel MDF *1.9(¾") x 122(4") x 244cm (8")*
- Single-thread multi-purpose wood screws
- Screws, washers and rawlplugs appropriate for your wall

* MDF : Medium Density Fibreboard

Telling details: The natural patina of the vintage crates is set off by a poplar surround.

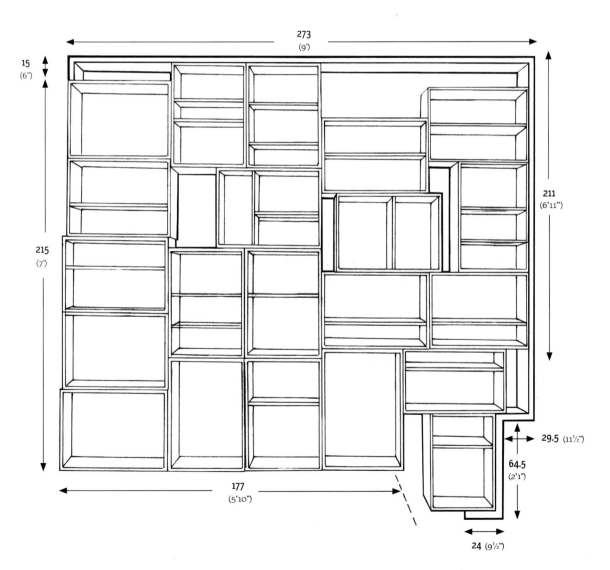

All measurements are given in centimetres and inches (to nearest fraction).

Step-by-step-guide

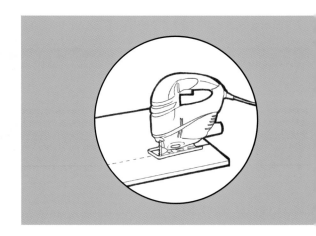

1. Wash down the crates with soda crystals dissolved in hot water (50g/.9oz per litre/pint), taking care not to soak the wood. Leave to dry completely.

2. To make the shelves, measure the internal dimensions of the crates and mark them on the MDF panel, then saw them out.

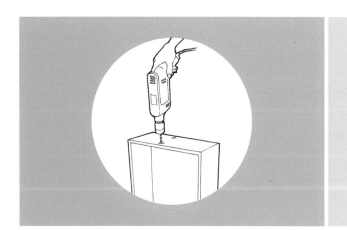

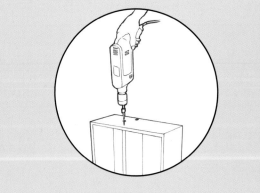

3. Mark the positions for the screws on the crates and pre-drill pilot holes. Vary the height of the shelves according to the sizes of your books.

4. Screw the shelves in place on both sides.

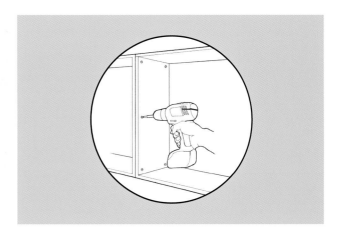

5. Try out different arrangements of the crates in order to decide their final positions.

6. Screw the crates together to ensure stability.

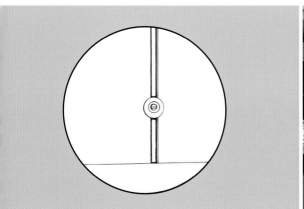

7. Fix some of the crates to the wall in order to ensure the construction stays upright. Use rawlplugs appropriate to your wall.

8. Here, to finish off the bookcase, a surround of melamine-faced poplar boards has been made-to-measure by a cabinetmaker.

Bookcase Staircase
LEVITATE/London

As part of their extension of a top-floor flat in a Victorian mansion block, LEVITATE created a new bedroom level in the unused loft space, reached by a 'secret' staircase hidden from the living room.

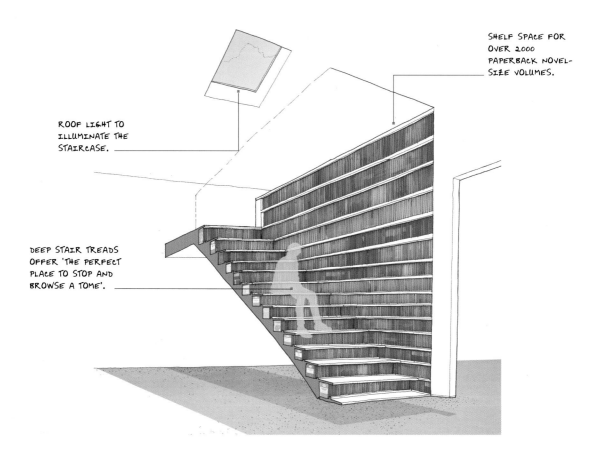

SHELF SPACE FOR OVER 2000 PAPERBACK NOVEL-SIZE VOLUMES.

ROOF LIGHT TO ILLUMINATE THE STAIRCASE.

DEEP STAIR TREADS OFFER 'THE PERFECT PLACE TO STOP AND BROWSE A TOME'.

Founded in 2005 by Tim Sloan and Spencer Guy, LEVITATE now employs an eleven-strong design-led team committed to 'designing sustainable and contextual contemporary architecture' in the form of 'spaces that function effectively and are a joy to be in.'

LEVITATE - Architecture & Design Studio
161 Rosebery Avenue - London, UK, EC1R 4QX
Tel: +44 (0)20 7833 4455
studio@levitate.uk.com/www.levitate.uk.com

Illuminated from above by a roof light, the English oak stair treads and shelves are completely lined with books.

WATSON

Watson is a classic of bookcase design.
Standing against a wall or set into a niche,
it is perfectly at home in any type of room.

Perfect for novices, this MDF project is extremely
simple to build and can easily be adapted to meet
all practical needs and aesthetic requirements.

DESIGN:
DANIEL LE MOAL

WATSON

TOOLBOX	
Tools	**Materials**
■ Metal set square ■ Screw gun ■ Spirit level ■ Small paint roller ■ Sash paintbrush	■ MDF, *20mm (¾")* for the shelves, *25mm (1")* for the structure *(here 5 sections of 27 (10½") x 250cm (8'2"); 2 of 27 (10½") x 232cm (7'7"); 1 of 10 (4") x 250cm (8'2"); 9 of 10 (4") x 19cm (7½"); 26 of 25 (9¾") x 50cm (1'8")* ■ Single-thread multi-purpose wood screws ■ 45 L-brackets *3 (1¼") x 3cm (1¼")* ■ 140 ø5mm (¹³/₆₄) nickel-plated steel bolts ■ Screws, washers and rawlplugs appropriate for your wall ■ Paint of your choice

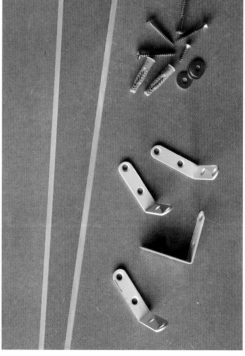

Telling details: The construction method for this bookcase is simplicity itself. The design is enlivened by the different heights of the shelves.

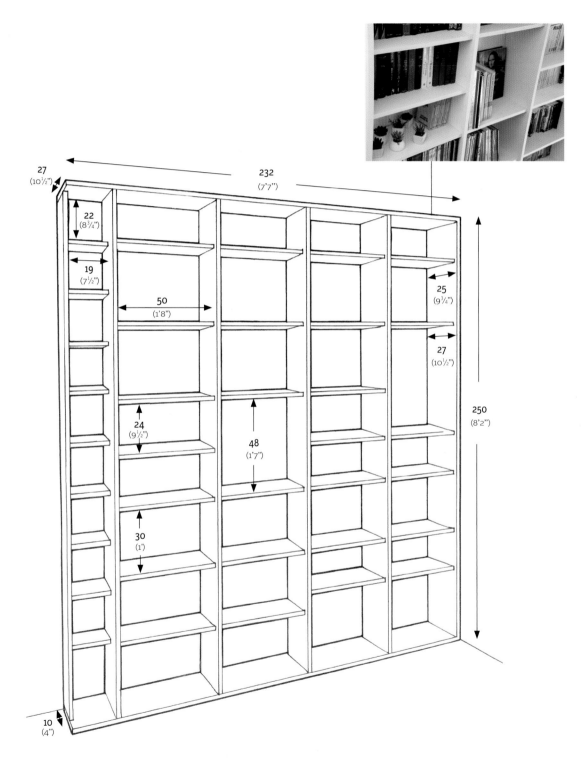

27
(10½")

232
(7'7")

22
(8¾")

19
(7½")

25
(9¾")

50
(1'8")

27
(10½")

24
(9½")

250
(8'2")

48
(1'7")

30
(1')

10
(4")

All measurements are given in centimetres and inches (to nearest fraction).

Step-by-step-guide

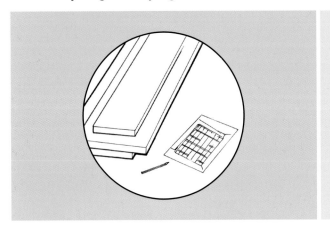

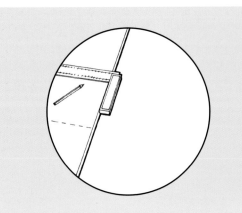

1. Make a scale drawing of your bookcase in order to work out the positions, depths, heights and widths of your shelves. Cut the shelves out of MDF.

2. Using a metal set square, mark the positions of the shelves on the uprights. Number your uprights to make this easier.

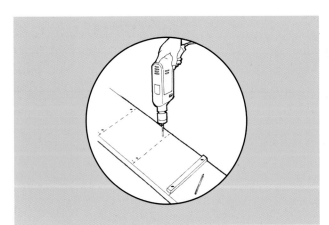

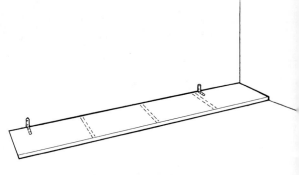

3. Take a length of batten and mark it with the positions of the two holes for the bolts. Hold this on the marked positions of the shelves to mark the position of the bolts. Drill blind holes. If you do not have a depth gauge, wrap a bit of sticky tape around the drill bit to mark the correct depth.

4. Place the bottom board (here measuring 27 (10½") x 232cm (7'7")) on the floor, hard up against the wall, and use brackets to fix it in position. Mark out the positions of the uprights.

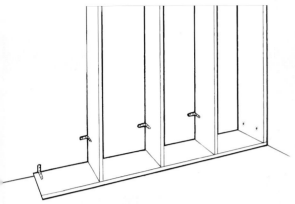

5. Fix the end upright (here 27 (10½") x 250cm (8'2") to the wall using the appropriate rawlplugs, then fix the other uprights with angle-brackets.

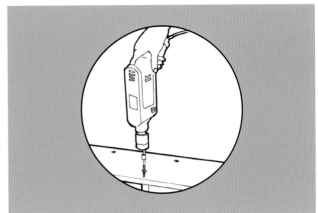

6. Screw the top board (here 27 (10½") x 232cm (7'7")) to each upright, pre-drilling the holes to prevent splitting.

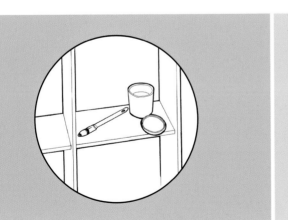

7. Apply 2 coats of paint to the whole structure, using a sash paintbrush for the angles and a small roller for the flat surfaces. Paint the shelves before putting them in position.

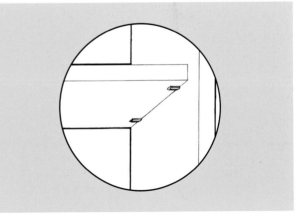

8. Put the shelves in position and insert the bolts. To finish, put a dab of paint on the ends of the bolts.

CONTEMPORAINE

INSPIRATION

When Frédérique had to decide where to put a bookcase, her office was the obvious choice.

Filling the whole of one wall, this bookcase is unusual for the sturdiness of its shelves and for their long horizontal lines. With its clean, uncluttered lines this design is strikingly graphic in its effect, while its sober wood finish lends it a timeless stylishness.

DESIGN:
FRÉDÉRIQUE SAMSON

CONTEMPORAINE

'Art, travel, decoration, architecture ... I love beautiful books, and I wanted a bookcase to keep them in. I also needed storage space for personal items that we didn't want to put on display, such as photograph albums. These were my two criteria in designing this piece, which also had to fit the dimensions of the room we chose for it, the office. This private space was the place that best suited our lifestyle. Wood seemed a natural choice, as it is both a warm material and ideal for creating a contemporary feel.

CLOSE-UP ON MATERIALS

VENEERED LAMINATE

This design uses laminate veneered in oak and stained grey. The thin oak veneer, cut along the grain, is glued to the chipboard panels that form the structure of the bookcase. Different types of wood can be used to create a variety of shades and visual appearances, like the contoured surface here. Combining low cost with high aesthetic value, this solution economizes on the use of expensive wood. Many manufacturers now offer a range of decorative products using wood veneers, with a range of colours and textures (worn, weathered, distressed, etc.) offering a wide choice for interior design projects.

370
(12'2")

6
(2½")

245
(8')

34
(1'1")

41
(1'4")

38
(1'3")

39
(1'4")

28
(11")

All measurements are given in centimetres and inches (to nearest fraction).

Construction

Made to measure by the joiners and cabinetmakers of Atelier Boutin, this horizontal bookcase plays on the dimensions of the room. The chunky shelves, are invisibly fixed and apparently unsupported along their full length. The back is purely aesthetic and serves no weight-bearing function. By economizing on materials, wood veneer offers high aesthetic values within a limited budget.

MAX. SHELF SPACE

With its long, uninterrupted shelves, the bookcase offers clear display and easy access for the books it holds. The average shelf height of 39cm (1'4") is designed to accommodate large format books. The contrast between the dark grey of the wood and the white of the walls emphasizes the linear character of the design.

INVISIBLE FIXINGS

To lighten the structure, the shelves are hung on the walls and there are no uprights. The invisible fixings screw into the wall and into the back of the shelves at 70cm (2'4") intervals.

ARCHIVE SPACE

In a solution that combines a bookcase with archive space, the lower part of the bookcase contains six drawers designed to hold photograph albums and other personal documents. The push-pull drawers have no handles, so contributing to the overall minimalist effect.

Frédérique Samson
Interior Designer

Frédérique in 5 dates
1990: Graduates from the Ecole Nationale Supérieure d'Architecture, Nantes.
1991: Beginning of a 20-year career in textiles, as director of collections and design for concept stores.
1999: Travels to Miami, where she discovers Philippe Starck's designs for the Delano South Beach Hotel.
2004: Creative director. She will later transfer the use of the concept board to her interior design work.
2012: Sets up her own interior design practice.

When she set up her own practice in 2012, Frédérique took the small step from the world of fashion to the world of interior design. Whether designing an interior or a fashion collection, the process — involving researches into materials, colours and shapes — is the same. 'Just as when I'm doing fashion design, I use a concept board to create the palette and atmosphere of a room.' Her signature style is clean and contemporary, with a warm note provided by the generous use of wood.

What are your tips for making a bookcase?
The way we view the lines of a piece of furniture is highly personal to each individual. For bookcases I put the emphasis on horizontal lines in order to avoid any feeling of compartmentalization. I try to avoid vertical uprights, as bookshelves quickly get filled up, leaving no breathing space. Using thick shelves to create strong horizontals helps to distinguish the bookcase from its surroundings and offers new perspectives on the space. I would also advise leaving the shelves open, and not closing them in with glass or any other material. They should be easy to reach, tempting you to take down a book. Open shelves are an invitation to read.

When it comes to putting your books on the shelves, be creative. Pile them up vertically as well as horizontally, but above all don't arrange them all in the same direction: try to break with the linear rhythm of traditional bookcases.

Tell us a favourite book.
Liaigre by Christian Liaigre and Thomas Luntz (Flammarion).

Frédérique Samson
Tel: +33 (0)6 03 11 07 00
contact@frederiquesamson.com
www.frederiquesamson.com

Contemporaine (p. 172)

APPENDICES

Diagrams
Address Book
Acknowledgements

HARLOTTE UP (see p. 77)

2 106 (3'6") x 106cm (3'6")
3-stringer pallets with overhanging deckboards

2 4-stringer reversible pallets

cuts

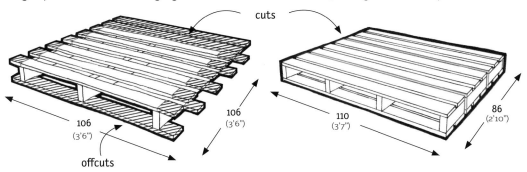

106
(3'6")

106
(3'6")

offcuts

110
(3'7")

86
(2'10")

2 sections with 3 boards

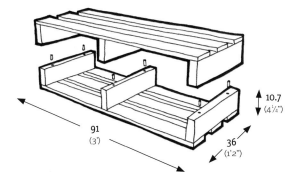

10.7
(4¼")

91
(3')

36
(1'2")

4 sections with 3 boards

2 sections with 2 boards

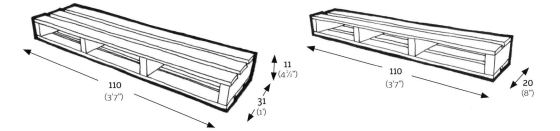

110
(3'7")

11
(4½")

31
(1')

110
(3'7")

20
(8")

All measurements are given in centimetres and inches (to nearest fraction).

GLOBE READER (see p. 41)

1 square = 10 cm (4")

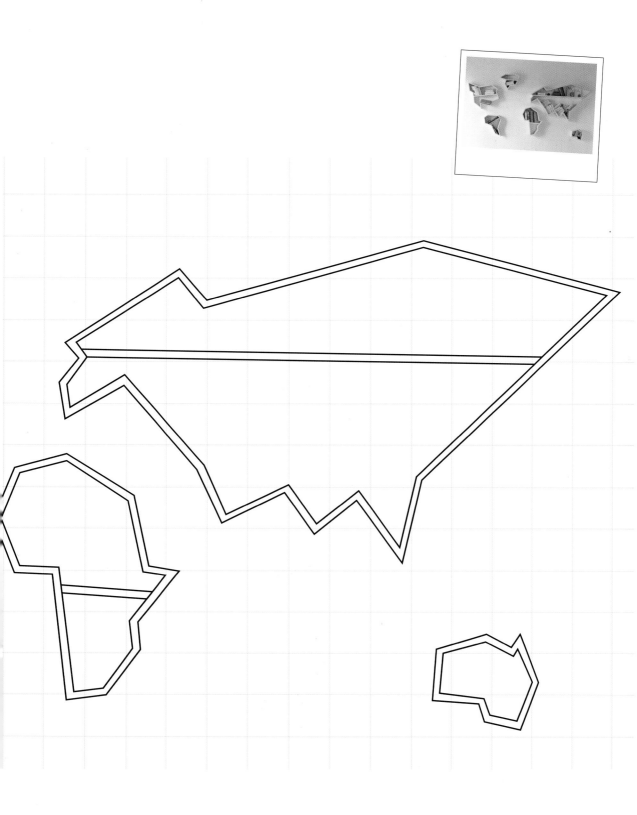

ADDRESS BOOK

DESIGNS

■ **BL Quincaillerie**
(threaded rods and screws, image p. 48)
www.blquincaillerie.com

■ **Bulle Créa Concept**
(long-stemmed poppies, image p. 64)
www.bullecreaconcept.fr

■ **Les Enfants du Brok/Traditional**
  & Industrial Homeware
(old bar stool and storage jar, image p. 104)
18, rue Gutenberg - 44100 Nantes, France
Tel: +33 (0)2 49 44 78 32
contact@lesenfantsdubrok.com
www.lesenfantsdubrok.com

■ **Denis Guitton/Designer-Antique dealer**
Beaupuy - 85480 Fougeré
Tel: +33 (0)6 64 24 76 60
guittondenis@yahoo.fr

■ **ETS Guillon Nicolas/Cabinetmaker & Joiner**
(poplar and white melamine surround, image p. 158)
217, rue du Puits-Abri-Méron
49260 Montreuil-Bellay, France
Tel: +33 (0)2 41 59 43 04/+33 (0)6 81 08 57 56
contact@menuiserie-guillon.com
www.menuiserie-guillon49.com

■ **Les M&M Designers**
  Martin Lévêque
44, rue Eeckelaers - 1210 Bruxelles, Belgium
Tel: +32 (0)4 85 78 55 19
martinlvqe@gmail.com/www.be.net/martinleveque

■ **Mathieu Maingourd**
massiouxx@gmail.com/www.be.net/math_ology

■ **Fanny Mercier/Freelance Creative Director**
fanny.mercier@gmail.com
www.fannymercier.fr/tetedange.canalblog.com

■ **Frédéric Mazère/Artiste peintre**
(paintings, images pp. 48 and 84)
10, rue Maurice-Terrien - 44100 Nantes

■ **La Passerelle de Marcel/Brasserie**
(image p. 8)
7, allée Jacques-Berque - Stade Marcel-Saupin
44100 Nantes, France
Tel: +33 (0)2 51 86 60 56
www.lapasserelledemarcel.com

■ **Jean-Marie Reymond/Designer**
6 bis, rue Noire - 44000 Nantes, France
Tel: +33 (0)2 40 48 54 96
jeanmariereymond@hotmail.com
www.behance.net/jdce

INSPIRATIONS

GRAPHIC DESIGN

■ **Atelier Premier Étage/**
  Interior designers
3, rue Victor-Letalle - 75020 Paris, France
Tel: +33 (0)6 03 69 53 94
claire.escalonlanno@gmail.com/www.premieretage.com

CONTEMPORAINE

■ **Atelier Boutin (image p. 172)**
ZI de la Chevrolière - 20, rue du Bois-Fleuri
44118 La Chevrolière, France
Tel: +33 (0)2 40 13 31 05/Paris : 06 80 13 39 00
ebenisterie@atelierboutin.com/www.atelierboutin.com

Beta-Plus Editions
(books on architecture, interior design and gardens)
www.betaplus.com

IDM
(Panton chair and Arco lamp, image p. 172)
2 rue de La-Noue-Bras-de-Fer - 44000 Nantes, France
: +33 (0) 2 40 47 01 47
www.espace-idm.com

Frédérique Samson
: +33 (0) 6 03 11 07 00
contact@frederiquesamson.com/www.frederiquesamson.com

Yellow Korner
(photographs, image p. 172)
www.yellowkorner.com

MULTI-LAYERED READINGS

Artazart/Design Bookstore
, quai de Valmy - 75010 Paris, France
www.artazart.com

Ich&Kar/Graphic designers
, rue du Sergent-Godefroy – 93100 Montreuil, France
www.ichetkar.fr

Lanno Design Paris
design and marketing, furniture, objets d'art and lighting
nicolas.lanno@gmail.com/www.nicolaslanno.com

SPIRIT OF INDUSTRY

Agence MGA architecte DPLG (Maureen Gâté)
bis, rue Albert-Ier - 92600 Asnières-sur-Seine, France
: +33 (0) 1 55 02 30 06
agence@mga-architectes.com/www.mga-architectes.com

Carl Hansen & Son
(HO7 chair by Hans J. Wegner, image p. 61)
www.carlhansen.com

■ Fatboy
(Buggle Up beanbag, image p. 56)
www.fatboy.com

■ GreenRiver/Building and construction projects
16 bis, rue Montaigne - 92600 Asnières-sur-Seine, France
contact@greenriver.fr/www.greenriver.fr

■ J&A Décoration/Renovation & decoration
2, rue Jean-Jaurès - 92270 Bois-Colombes, France
contact@ja-decoration.com/www.ja-decoration.com

■ NUD Collection
(NUD Exclusive pendant light, image p. 61)
www.nudcollection.com

IN THE RAW

■ Bulle Créa Concept
Christophe Potet
Tel: +33 (0) 6 31 03 05 70
christophe.potet@bullecreaconcept.fr
www.bullecreaconcept.fr

■ Moulinsart
(Tintin bust and rocket, image p. 90)
www.tintinboutique.com

RECTO-VERSO

■ h2o architectes
24, place Raoul-Follereau - 75010 Paris, France
Tel: +33 (0) 9 64 00 52 81
contact@h2oarchitectes.com/www.h2oarchitectes.com

DESIGNER PROFILES

BOOKCASE STAIRCASE

- **LEVITATE - Architecture & Design Studio**
161, Rosebery-Avenue - London EC1R 4QX, UK
Tel: +44 (0)20 7833 4455
studio@levitate.uk.com/www.levitate.uk.com

THE STAIRCASE AS FURNITURE

- **Marc Koehler Architects**
Keizersgracht 126 - 1015 cw Amsterdam, Holland
Tel: +31 (0)20 575 5508
office@marckoehler.nl/www.marckoehler.nl

LITERARY ENCOUNTERS

- **Shakespeare and Company**
37, rue de la Bûcherie - 75005 Paris, France
Tel: +33 (0)1 43 25 40 93
news@shakespeareandcompany.com
www.shakespeareandcompany.com

TREME-TREME

- **Triptyque**
38, rue de Rochechouart - 75009 Paris, France
Tel: +33 (0)1 75 43 42 16
Al. Gabriel Monteiro da Silva, 484
01442-000 São Paulo, Brazil

BODY AND SOUL!

- **Cook & Book**
1, place du Temps-Libre
1200 Woluwé-Saint-Lambert, Belgium
Tel: +32 (0) 2 761 26 00
www.cookandbook.com

PHOTOGRAPHERS

- **Jérôme Blin**
jerome.blin22@yahoo.fr/www.bellavieza.com

- **Cédric Chassé (photo p. 8)**
c2rix@free.fr/http://c2rix.free.fr

- **Céline Clanet (photo p. 114–119)**
contact@celineclanet.com/www.celineclanet.com

- **Leonardo Finotti (photo p. 46)**
photo@leonardofinotti.com/www.leonardofinotti.com

- **Marcel van der Burg (photo p. 142)**
primabeeld@gmail.com/www.primabeeld.nl

WEBSITES

- **Bookstore Guide**
'An amateur guide to book shopping throughout Europe.'
www.bookstoreguide.org

- **Bookshelf**
'The home of interesting bookshelves, bookcases and things that
look like them.'
www.theblogonthebookshelf.blogspot.fr

- **Bookshelf Porn**
'A photoblog created to allow people to indulge their love of book
libraries, bookstores and bookcases by showcasing the best
bookshelf photos from around the world.'
.http://bookshelfporn.com

- **Chiara Stella Home**
Lifestyle and inspirations.
www.blog.chiara-stella-home.com/diy-une-bibliotheque-facile-a-
realiser
see also: http://lescats.over-blog.com/categorie-10611819.html

- **Igota**
Step-by-step guide to building a Tetris bookcase.
www.igota.fr/pages/realiser-un-meuble-en-blocs-tetris

La Cité du Livre
The spectacular Cité du Livre project in Aix-en-Provence.
www.citedulivre-aix.com

Mathieu Gabiot
Step-by-step guide to the Nonpareille bookcase.
www.mathieu-g.be/fr/2012/09/nonpareille/

Musée des arts et métiers du livre - Musée Michel-Faibant
www.montolieu-livre.fr

The Brick House
Step-by-step guide to making a pipe shelving unit.
www.the-brick-house.com/2009/09/shelving-unit
The varitions on this theme:
http://thestyleeater.com
http://manhattan-nest.com/2010/10/20/pipe-ply/

Underground New York Public Library
'visual library featuring the Reading-Riders of the NYC subways.'
www.undergroundnewyorkpubliclibrary.com

Forgotten Books
The World's largest online library.
www.forgottenbooks.com

The Millions
The world's most popular online literary magazine.
www.themillions.com

Page-Turner
The New Yorker's online book blog.
www.newyorker.com/books/page-turner

The Public Domain review
An online journal and not-for-profit project dedicated
to promoting and celebrating the public domain in all
its richness and variety.
http://publicdomainreview.org/

The Book Cover Archive
An online archve of book covers by Designer, Publisher, Author,
Title, and much more...
http://bookcoverarchive.com/

■ Goodreads
Goodreads is the world's largest site for readers and book
recommendations. Our mission is to help people find and share
books they love.
http://www.goodreads.com/

ACKNOWLEDGEMENTS

Our thanks go to all the designers and architects who collaborated on this book for their generous help and advice.
To the project owners for their warm welcome during on-site photography, and to all those who have helped to make this book possible.

CREDITS

PHOTOGRAPHS

All photographs are by Jérôme Blin, with the following exception:,

- p. 8   Cédric Chassé
- p. 26   Fanny Mercier
- p. 46   Leonardo Finotti/Beto Consorte
- p. 72 & 180   by 2 PHOTOGRAPHERS/Frédéric Sablon
- p. 102   Shakespeare and Company Paris Archive, 1979–1980/
                  Shoshan/Thomas Pirel
- p. 114–119   Céline Clanet
- p. 142   Marcel Van Der Burg
- p. 164   LEVITATE

ILLUSTRATIONS
Jean-Marie Reymond

DECORS
Aurélie Drouet & Jérôme Blin

STYLING
Aurélie Drouet

Published by **Scriptum Editions**, 2015

An imprint of **Co & Bear Productions (UK) Ltd**

63 Edith Grove, London, SW10 0LB

www.scriptumeditions.co.uk

PUBLISHERS: **Beatrice Vincenzini & Francesco Venturi**

COVER DESIGN: **Mr Cat**

TRANSLATION: **Barbara Mellor**

EDITORIAL: **Juliette de Lavaur, Françoise Mathay & Marion Dellapina**

GRAPHIC DESIGN: **Gaëlle Chartier, Sabine Houplain, Claire Mieyeville & Audrey Lorel**

Distributed by **Thames & Hudson**

10 9 8 7 6 5 4 3 2 1

ISBN: **978–1–902686–82-0**

First published, in French, by **Editions du Chêne – Hachette Livre, 2013**

Original title: ***100% Déco: Bibliothèques, faites vos meubles***

©**Editions du Chêne – Hachette Livre, 2013**, for the original work.

Translation ©**Co&Bear Productions (UK) Ltd**